W9-AQD-032

MINDING
YOUR
BUSINESS

MINDING YOUR BUSINESS

A Guide to Money and Taxes for Creative Professionals

MARTIN KAMENSKI

Hal Leonard Books

An Imprint of Hal Leonard Corporation

Published in 2013 by Hal Leonard Books
An Imprint of Hal Leonard Corporation
7777 West Bluemound Road
Milwaukee, WI 53213

Trade Book Division Editorial Offices
33 Plymouth St., Montclair, NJ 07042

IMAGE CREDITS
iStockphoto: I-1, I-2, I-3, 1-3, 2-1, 2-7, 3-6, 3-8, 4-1, 4-2, 4-3, 5-1, 6-1, 6-4
IRS/Martin Kamenski: 1-1, 1-2, 2-2, 2-3, 2-6, 3-2, 5-2
Martin Kamenski: 2-4, 2-5, 2-8, 3-1, 3-3, 3-4, 3-5, 3-7, 3-9, 3-10, 4-4, 5-3, 6-2, 6-3

Printed in The United States of America

Book design by Michael Kellner

Library of Congress Cataloging-in-Publication Data
Kamenski, Martin.
 Minding your business : a guide to money and taxes for creative professionals / Martin Kamenski.
    pages cm
 Includes bibliographical references.
 1. Self-employed. 2. Bookkeeping. 3. Artisans--Taxation. I. Title.
 HD8036.K36 2012
 658.15--dc23
                        2012033826

ISBN 978-1-4584-3785-3

www.halleonardbooks.com

Contents

Foreword

You are holding a very important book in your hands.

As a professional marketer, publicist, and advocate who has dedicated my entire adult life to helping artists, I can think of no one better to write the introduction for this book, because if there is one thing that artists hate (aside from marketing and publicity), it's the money conversation and story.

This book will empower you to lose the story that a vast majority of artists who wish to live their dreams have been telling themselves for years.

"What story?" you ask.

This one: in our society, we are taught to believe that in order to be really good at art that expresses our real talent, our passions, our hearts and souls, and our joy, we are not allowed to profit from it.

And if we are lucky enough to profit from it, others around us may not be profiting from it, and therefore we feel shame, guilt, embarrassment, and discomfort.

Perhaps we make money from a dream that parents and peers and friends told us we couldn't have, so of course the money piece becomes confusing, overwhelming, or something that you might have pushed off to the side.

Martin Kamenski, a calm, collected, and wise teacher, will help you confront these issues in the pages of this book.

Martin is a kindred spirit. Being an advisor and practitioner to creatives is a highly rewarding career but is often fraught with confronting other people's said stories (read: fears). Martin has a deep capacity for calm, clear, collected conversation and advice.

This is expressed throughout this book, and you will feel much more like a dear friend is taking you by the hand and leading you through the morass than a "CPA" (although he is a highly qualified CPA). Most importantly, he is a rare CPA because he speaks "artist."

As a creative entrepreneur, I learned so much from reading this book and appreciate its straightforward and kind delivery; I know that you will too.

So go forth without fear, pick up some tips that you might not have learned or known, and from now on, make better financial choices and take more responsibility around your art as your business.

Martin has minded your business with such detail and kindness that after reading this book, you have the possibility of getting back to minding more of your art.

And the best part: this book is your first write-off in the next (tax) chapter of your new life.

—Ariel Hyatt

Acknowledgments

I'd like to take a moment here to thank a number of people who were instrumental in making this book happen.

- Mica, Mia, Ava, and Zora Kamenski: the loving family that has supported my efforts every step of the way and without whom nothing would be possible. Much love to my girls.
- Michael and Sherri Kamenski, Maria Gesiorek: the proud parents who have supported me from day one.
- John Cerullo: the man at Hal Leonard Publishing who saw value in bringing this resource to the artistic community.
- Celina Rivera: my right hand at Rockstar CPA and the glue that binds my work together.
- Greg Peterca, Donald Lawrence, and Quietwater Entertainment LLC: our neighbors, friends, and family. Thank you for believing in and supporting Rockstar CPA for years and years.
- New Wave Coffee: providing the essential fuel that allowed for my late-night writing sessions.
- Ariel Hyatt: who graciously offered the foreword to this book and whose contribution to helping artists promote their careers has empowered the independent music scene.
- The amazing, talented, and inspiring clients of Rockstar CPA. Your questions have given this book the skeleton of its structure, and your faith in our work has fleshed out its body. It's a privilege to be at your service.

Introduction

THE PURPOSE OF THE BOOK

What It Is and What It Is Not

If there's anything a creative person tends to dislike more than talking about money, it's talking about taxes. But paying attention to the business of your art is an important craft itself. Whether you are a graphic designer or painter, sound effect artist or videographer, author or ·musician, film production studio or record label, your business and your art are inextricably intertwined. You see this as you move through your daily life: the book you're reading for

Figure I-1

fun that suddenly spurs an idea for your next project, the lunch meeting that winds up landing you a new contract, the cell phone that tracks every aspect of your personal *and* your work life.

The goal of this book is to give you some perspective on how income, expenses, and taxes can flow through your work without trouble. Along the way, several myths will be dispelled and fears quelled. As you read, be sure to jot your questions down at the end on the "Notes" page and then cross them out if they're subsequently answered. If not, feel free to submit them at http://www.rockstarcpa.com/minding-your-business, and I will get back to you with answers.

But more importantly, here's what the book is not. This book is not going to walk you through a tax return. There are plenty of guides out there that do a good enough job pointing you to which numbers go on which lines. This book is also not an attempt to list every potentially tax-deductible expense. Why? Because as you'll read in the section called "The Golden Rule of Deductions," it's literally impossible to come up with any exhaustive list.

It's not possible to address every possible scenario that you as a creative professional might face. Others have tried, and it's often not pretty. Instead, I will have faith and confidence in you and your creative spirit. Read the examples, and think about how they might apply to what you are trying to do. Odds are good that although you may be making money in your own unique way, there are still commonalities with your creative peers.

Instead this book will focus on teaching you principles you can understand and apply over and over. It will teach you to think about what you do in a way that is both empowering and efficient. It will help you examine how you work: how you make money, how you spend money, and how best to minimize your taxes. It will end your fear of taxes and the IRS, and help you lead the life you crave as a creative professional.

Other Good Books to Use Along with It

There are many books that have been written about artists, and even more that are written about taxes. Combing through them all to find the most valuable gems can be an arduous endeavor, and as a thank you for grabbing *this* particular book off the shelf, your search will now be a whole lot easier. There are no pretenses regarding publishing alliances, no cross-promotional gimmicks. These are simply the most helpful books for creative individuals looking to take their business seriously, along with a brief synopsis of each.

The Wealthy Freelancer (Available Here: http://bit.ly/y3iRl1)

This book by Steve Slaunwhite and Pete Savage discusses many aspects of the "freelance lifestyle." They contend that these days more than ever, people are finding themselves working on their own—a stance you'll see echoed in this book. But what got this book an enthusiastic endorsement was the manner in which it handles two key questions that plague so many self-employed and freelance individuals. The first is, "How do I price my time/work?" This question may have surfaced for you as, "Should I bill hourly or per project?" or "Is it dangerous to price myself *too* competitively?" The second question they attack is how to choose the right projects to work on. Talk to any seasoned self-employed artist or creative, and they will *all* have stories for you about the perils of agreeing to the wrong project. Choosing wisely is arguably one of the most important business decisions you will make on a regular basis. *The Wealthy Freelancer* will help you construct a framework for the long haul.

The Money Book (Available Here: http://bit.ly/PPmEIB)

Cash flow can be one of the biggest challenges to those taking the self-employed route. The path of traditional employment often comes with a steady paycheck, taxes withheld every step of the way, and even refunds from time to time. Freelance or self-employed artists and creatives often face years with spotty incoming cash flow (royalty checks here and there, uncertain work future, large checks that have to last you a long time) and little to no taxes withheld on their behalf. While *Minding Your Business* will educate you enough to know the landscape—the paths of least resistance, the dangerous pitfalls of misinformation, the smartest shortcuts—*The Money Book* by Joseph D'Agnese and Denise Kiernan will help you take whatever your eventual cash flow needs are and generate a real-life workable money plan. In plain language, no frills. Certainly a worthy companion on your journey.

Brains on Fire (Available Here: http://bit.ly/wOiliP)

Though not specifically for self-employed individuals, this book by Robbin Phillips and the folks of consulting firm Brains on Fire is critical to understanding the changes in today's marketing practices. If your understanding of how to sell your product (or yourself, if that's your biggest asset!) still revolves around price, product, place, and promotion, you are missing out on a truly remarkable way to engage with your customers. These days, whether you are an actor trying to land an audition, a band trying to ramp up to the next level, a writer trying to publish your first e-zine, or a photographer with your own successful studio, the single most important way to grow your business is through connecting with your customers—in a real and memorable way. That's it. And *Brains on Fire* is the perfect guidebook to show you how. It's packed with ideas that will help you build relationships with your target audience and help you become fans of your fans. You won't find much of a discussion about marketing yourself in *Minding Your Business*—as important as that is for any artist or creative professional. Instead, I suggest you read *Brains on Fire*.

Built to Sell (Available Here: http://bit.ly/wfRdRv)

John Warrillow wrote a book that is a must-read for any developing service-based business. Not necessarily one for the actors and musicians in the crowd to pick up, but for the photographers, web designers, graphic design shops, and printing companies, this book will without a doubt change the way you think about your business. You needn't be in a place where you're looking to sell your business at present. It doesn't matter. What *does* matter is that you probably would at least like the option to sell it someday. Just *the option*. And this book will help you avoid making the mistakes that so many owners of service-based businesses make. Instead, it will teach you how to free yourself—the creative overseer—from the day-to-day operations of the business so that it could conceivably live on without you. Because without that, you will have put years into your business only to have created *your own job* and nothing more. Learn what gives a business value. And then build that into your plan for development. Walk away satisfied.

Online Resources to Note

There are a number of online resources that can help you with various elements of your creative business, from getting it started to prepping for taxes. Though this listing will be out of date almost as soon as it's published (thus is the nature of our ever-expanding Internet), I thought it would be helpful to list a few resources that I pass along to my clients on a regular basis.

Figure I-2

- **GETTING STARTED**
  - **IRS (http://www.irs.gov):** The IRS is where you will go to obtain a tax ID number (TIN) or employer identification number (EIN) for your activity. They also have a large bank of information about being self-employed or incorporated. Anything you find on their site is valid proof of how you handle things for yourself (should anyone ever question you).
  - **GoDaddy (http://godaddy.com):** Though there are a number of services out there that will let you reserve your domain name and provide hosting for your site, none seem to provide quite the "full package" of support—from managing multiple sites to e-commerce and QuickBooks integration—that GoDaddy does. Especially if you're looking to start a business with a name other than your own name, it's a good idea to check first if you can get the website URL you want.
  - **Local Secretary of State (Varies, but It's Searchable):** Once you know that you have the website you want, it's time to check with your local secretary of state to make sure you can obtain the rights to that name within your state. The secretary of state is only allowed to have one active registration under any given name, so it's important to check here as well before you get your website and bank accounts lined up. If you can't incorporate under the name you want, you might have to get creative.
  - **US Patent and Trademark Office (http://uspto.gov):** Even once you have things squared away with your website and the local secretary of state, your name is not protected nationwide until you apply for a trademark or servicemark. The USPTO registers all names of businesses nationwide and does a thorough search for "competitive confusion." The idea is that you can't set up a name that might be mistaken for another business—even if

it's not exactly the same name—if a consumer might mistake your business for the other. For example, if "Jiffy Time Design" is registered as a web design firm, they will probably not let you register "Jiffy Web Design," as the two could easily be confused. But on the flipside, you'll benefit from the same level of protection when it comes to your registered name.

○ **Is Incorporating Right for Me? (http://bit.ly/LtP0QP):** In 2011, we wrote this short primer on the simple questions surrounding incorporation. It would be safe to say that almost everything discussed is already covered in the various sections of *Minding Your Business*, but if you'd like it in a bite-sized e-book format, you can pick this up for a gentle reminder of the finer points of making this decision.

• **KEEPING UP OPERATIONS**

○ **Outright (http://bit.ly/Jy1wxU):** This web-based bookkeeping platform is perfect for the self-employed artist or creative. It automates 95 percent of the data entry process, leaving you just needing to tag expenses with a category. A great time saver, and with a subscription of $10/month, it will keep track of your self-employment tax obligations for you so you're never shocked by another tax bill again.

○ **Freshbooks (http://bit.ly/LbJvGL):** Another simple web-based bookkeeping system that's a better fit for simple businesses. Though only recently a full-fledged accounting system, it can be a great starting ground before you jump into QuickBooks. Users who like a "Web 2.0" feel will be right at home with Freshbooks.

○ **QuickBooks (http://bit.ly/J9CaqC):** This is the grandfather of all modern accounting systems. With the biggest user base and longest operational history, there's very little that the makers of QuickBooks haven't considered yet. If you're not incorporated, it may be a little overkill, but once you've crossed that bridge into setting up your own corporation, it will be your go-to tool for tracking income and expenses.

○ **Harvest (http://getharvest.com):** For those who need to track their time in order to bill it back to their clients, there is no simpler available-on-every-platform system than Harvest. Whether you are out jogging with your phone in hand or poring over your laptop at the café, you'll be able to log every minute and track it back to the specific project you're working on. It has great tie-ins to other services as well.

○ **TaxTracker (http://bit.ly/ROZkdN):** Those of you with "smart" phones will love this handy app we've built to tackle two main challenges faced by all our creative clients: tracking receipts and tracking mileage. So forget stuffing those receipts in pockets, gig bags, or purses. Just take out your phone, snap a picture, tag it with a category, and the app reads all the other valuable information right off the receipt. Toss the paper. Simple as that. And while driving around, use the GPS in your phone to track the mileage for you. Because while you might not always have a paper and pen handy to log your miles, you're probably carrying your phone, right? Click the link to watch some videos about how it works.

• **MAKING TAX PAYMENTS**
   ○ **EFTPS (http://eftps.gov):** Though most payments to the IRS can be made by mail using a check, occasionally you'll need to send a payment online. Maybe you waited until the last minute. Or maybe it's a payment too large to send by check. The EFTPS system is the only electronic tax payment system actually run by the US government. You can pay any kind of individual or business taxes with it by electronic draft on your bank account. *N.B. You will*

need to have your account set up well in advance of making the payment (they send a secret code to your address by postcard, which takes some time), so it's best to get this set up right away so it's there for you when you need it.

o **Official Payments (http://www.officialpayments.com):** Though the IRS won't *directly* take payments by credit card, there is a way to rack up those miles just by paying your taxes. Official Payments is a licensed third-party gateway that will charge your credit card and forward the proceeds along to the IRS or your state department of revenue. Just be aware, they charge a fee for the service, so make sure to use their fee estimator before you proceed to be sure it's worth the expense to you.

There will be other resources brought up throughout the text, so keep your eyes open. And if you find others that would make good additions, mention them here: http://www.rockstarcpa.com/minding-your-business, and I'll be sure to add them to my next edition.

SO WHAT WILL WE TALK ABOUT?
How to Read

The best way to read this book is with a mind open to the various topics covered, but also focused in on the specific questions you might have about your career or business. It might be worthwhile to jot down your key questions in advance so your mind prepares to look for the answers throughout the text. The book can be viewed as a "crash course" in business and taxes for creatives if read in its entirety, or as a quick-reference guide to specific questions you have. Lastly, the case studies and review questions included are meant to aid professors and instructors at creative institutes of learning in using this text as a part of a final class or workshop prior to sending their artistic students into the working world. Those of you reading this in e-book format will have the added advantage of clicking straight out of the text, as I've enabled all websites as active hyperlinks in the text.

I wish there were a way to equate this whole endeavor—learning about the business of being an artist—to the beautiful process of creation that each of you go through on a daily basis. I struggled with metaphor after metaphor, but the fact is that this is not a very creative process. There are basic rules that you need to learn, and those rules have to be applied to how you handle yourself in the day-to-day work you do. But it's a necessary part of supporting any creative career, whether you are going to be a life-long freelancer or you are an owner of a gallery. It's the maintenance of your machine that will allow you the freedom to continue earning a living doing what you love. And that alone should be motivation enough.

Throughout the course of reading, it's my goal that you are able to correctly identify whether what you're doing is a business or a hobby, to know the difference between employees and independent contractors, to assess the right structure to suit your activity, to track your income and expenses, to keep track of your tax-filing obligations, to deal with the IRS (if you should be so lucky), and to put together a team that will support you in your endeavors. Lofty goals, yes. But I will chunk it out bit by bit and help you think through each of these topics in due course.

There is no wrong way to approach this book, but it can be rather dense material. Every effort has been taken to discuss things in a plain-language and easily logical fashion, but at the end of the day, I am talking about complicated matters and important decisions to make about your career. Take breaks when needed, and try to place yourself in the shoes of those discussed in the case studies. You'll have opportunities to take notes along the way, and also to ask me follow-up questions via my website. Enjoy.

Tools You Will Need

When you are thinking about the topics covered and how they may affect you, it's important to consider both where you're coming from and where you're going. It often takes a lot of work and money to undo or redo a part of the setup process. That's why I encourage people to read this book as soon as they start seriously thinking of an artistic career. I recall meeting with a client once who got word of her first big project out of college—she was getting hired for a long run on a Broadway tour of a musical. She was going to be making good money for a while, and someone on the cast recommended she set up an LLC. Someone else told her that she ought to incorporate in a state with no state income tax, such as Texas. She went online, paid $100 plus filing fees to have an online website draft up her paperwork, and thought she was set. Months later, someone recommended she speak to an accountant, and she found herself in my office. After talking through the considerations (many of which you'll come across in this book), it became apparent that an S-corporation set up in her home state would actually save her the most money. By jumping the gun, she wound up paying over $1,000 in fees to undo what she didn't need to do in the first place.

Likewise, it's important to think about where things are going. For example, you might not be in a position where incorporation makes a lot of sense for you right now. But it may be very likely beneficial in less than two years. Rather than fully set your bank accounts and build up habits as a sole proprietor, it would most likely make sense to go ahead and set up the business structure that will serve you best in the near future. I remember a couple who came in with a large project they were excited to take on, and when we talked about the income they were expecting, it became apparent that an S-corporation would be a good fit for them. But further talk brought to light the fact that they were going back to grad school in a year or two. It wasn't worth going through the process to set up the business for them when we would most likely need to tear it down again very soon.

Figure I-3

So when you get ready to put yourself in the shoes of those in the examples in this book, I recommend you gather up a bunch of paper and calculator, or an iPad, or whatever you like, and think about the following elements of your own situation. It will be most helpful to you if you're able to look at the examples presented and use your own information. Plug your own numbers into my math and see how these concepts would play out in your life.

1. **What *have you been* doing professionally?** What are you currently doing in your creative or artistic career? How are you accounting for that right now? Do you typically pay taxes at the end of the year or get refunds? Are you paid mostly as an employee or as an independent contractor?

2. **How *will you be* making your money as an artist in the near future?** What can you expect to bring in over the next 12 months? What about the 12 months after that? Do you have any sense of the kind of work you'll be doing? Will taxes be taken out?

3. **What are your work-related expenses like?** What kinds of things do you typically spend money on? Is your creative income turned around and entirely spent on those projects? Are you netting a profit? Or a loss?

4. **What other kinds of things impact your taxes?** Grab a tax return or two, the last couple that you filed. What other factors will impact your taxes? Do you rent or own? Do you have kids or not? If you have been doing whatever you do for some time, a tax return will give you an excellent barometer to determine if you are on the right path for your artistic career.

Decoding the Text

Throughout the text, you will see three important markings to act as guidelines for you and to call out the most important concepts. These are not revolutionary methods of presenting in a book, but I thought I'd take a quick second to call out each one so you know what you're looking at.

KEY POINT

Whenever I touch upon something particularly poignant or nugget-worthy, I'll call it out for you as a "Key Point." These are also meant to be a great refresher for you years after you put this book down the first time. Just zip through and reread all those key points, and you will have a good sense of the main topics addressed in the book. Or jot them down in a place of inspiration or where you keep track of your money to remind you of the goals and new practices you want to put into place.

CASE STUDY

The case studies throughout the book are meant to provide you with a more in-depth analysis of a particular concept. As I said, this material can be a bit dense at times, and real-world examples go a long way. Almost every example in this book is 100 percent true and taken straight from experiences I've had with my clients over the years. They are sometimes illustrative, and sometimes meant to drive home a point or to show the possible results of a particular course of action. These are excellent opportunities to put yourself in the driver's seat of the book. Try to go through each case study by equating it with what you're trying to do to see how it might affect your life. I wish I could have taken the time to use every particular creative profession as an example here, but life is short. So we'll rely a bit on the creativity and imagination that I know you all have.

STUDY QUESTIONS

Wait a minute . . . homework? Well, not really. These questions can certainly be used in a classroom or workshop setting. Or they can be used in a group reading setting for everyone to talk about how they might apply the information presented. But more than anything, they are meant to help you solidify the material and ensure that you understand. Could you skip them altogether? Sure. But when you're talking about things like money and taxes, better safe than sorry, right? So I'm helping you drive it home in as many ways as possible. I'll leave it to your judgment to use the methods that suit you best. On to the heart of the matter.

1

The "Business"

LIFE AS A CREATIVE PROFESSIONAL

There is something special that occurs when you get the opportunity to do what you love every day—and get paid for it. Studies show that less that 3 percent of Americans fit that bill, so you can count yourself in elite company. But there can be some unexpected downsides to making your passion your job. My clients come to me from all different places in life and looking to do all different things. Maybe you too are:

- fresh out of school
- recently laid off
- thinking about leaving an "employee job"
- going through a midlife career shift
- now receiving financial support of some kind

and are now:

- looking to get hired out as an independent contractor
- eager to open your own creative small business
- ready to partner with a few other talented individuals
- curious about what it's like to be self-employed
- freed up financially and able to explore your passion

No matter where you are coming from or what you are trying to do, there will undoubtedly be questions surrounding your transition. And it will be an exciting time when you are bursting with ideas and creativity and ready to hit the ground running. I want you to take some of that energy and apply it to working through this book. My goal is to arm you with the tools and information you need to get 50 percent of the way to a successful creative career. Your hard work and talent will get you the rest of the way there.

So let's take a moment to pause and reflect on what we're setting out to do here. Start with envisioning your ideal day. What are you doing? Who are you with? How are you exploring your talents? And imagine how it would feel to safely and successfully do that day after day. Those who are most successful in their creative careers acknowledge that their life—and they, themselves—are a business. It's the business that acts as a vehicle to carry you down the path to a life of pursuing your passions. That is why the proper setup and maintenance of your business is so important. And I am going to fill your toolbox with all the tips and tricks I can to make your journey successful.

ARE YOU A BUSINESS?

Before we talk about income or expenses, or LLCs and S-corporations, we ought to start with something basic. Some may view art and money as Republicans and Democrats: constantly at odds with each other, yet one could not exist without the other. And that view may be largely accurate, depending on your personal experiences. Art-making and creative professions (from editing to design to visual art) are an ever-growing segment of the US economy. And yet much creative work in the United States is still supported by public funding. So although in the real world, money and creativity live in this state of necessary balance, almost *nobody* likes to think about the business of making art. If you are a part of this majority, it's time to change your perspective.

The unfortunate circumstance is that as noble, romantic, or pure as your intentions may be, the only person you are short-changing by ignoring the business side of what you do is yourself. You may think it's acceptable, that the sacrifices are worth not having to taint your artistic pursuits with thoughts of the almighty dollar. But over a long enough career, most artists find at some point that making money itself is not an "impure" motive. It's not inherently bad. And you should not feel bad about making it. How much you can make is not the subject of this book. That will be left to market forces, your ability to promote yourself, and of course, the quality of your work. Instead, once you've made this money, this book will help you keep as much of it as possible—also a noble cause.

So if you'll permit a discussion of your creative practice as a business, the next phase is to learn why I want *the IRS* to see you as a business. There's a simple rule here: for-profit, business activities are allowed to deduct their losses against income made from other sources. How does this work? Well, here's an example:

Income	7 Wages, salaries, tips, etc. Attach Form(s) W-2	7	7,051.
	8a **Taxable** interest. Attach Schedule B if required	8a	
Attach Form(s)	b **Tax-exempt** interest. **Do not** include on line 8a	8b		
W-2 here. Also	9a Ordinary dividends. Attach Schedule B if required	9a	
attach Forms	b Qualified dividends.	9b		
W-2G and 1099-R	10 Taxable refunds, credits, or offsets of state and local income taxes.	10	0.
if tax was withheld.	11 Alimony received.	11	
If you did not	12 Business income or (loss). Attach Schedule C or C-EZ	12	-9,534.
get a W-2,	13 Capital gain or (loss). Att Sch D if reqd. If not reqd, ck here . . . . ▶ ☐	13	
see instructions.	14 Other gains or (losses). Attach Form 4797	14	
	15a IRA distributions	15a		b Taxable amount	15b	19,000.
	16a Pensions and annuities . . .	16a		b Taxable amount	16b	
Enclose, but do	17 Rental real estate, royalties, partnerships, S corporations, trusts, etc. Attach Schedule E	17	
not attach, any	18 Farm income or (loss). Attach Schedule F	18	
payment. Also,	19 Unemployment compensation	19	14,034.
please use	20a Social security benefits	20a		b Taxable amount	20b	
Form 1040-V.	21 Other income	21	
	22 Combine the amounts in the far right column for lines 7 through 21. This is your **total income** . . . . ▶	22	30,551.

Figure 1-1

The net effect of this all is that when your self-employed creative activity (dancing, painting, modeling) happens to spend more money than it brings in—and don't worry, this happens at some point to almost everyone—you'll be able to offset that against the income you made from your "day job." Or your rummage sale. Or your *other* self-employed activity. This has obvious advantages in reducing your overall income *and* your tax bill for the current year—which only makes sense! You *did* after all spend more money than you took in; no sense in paying taxes on money you already spent, right?

But what is the alternative? The alternative is being classified as a hobby. And all the rules will change. So let's talk about how and when classification as a hobby can ruin your year.

THE FIVE-YEAR RULE

Five years is a long time. It's a long time to know someone, it's a long time to be doing something. It's a long time to be hoping for something that never shows up. That's why when you start out by telling the IRS that you are a for-profit creative business activity (which again, you *will* do so you can offset any losses that occur), and you lose money for five years in a row, they will turn around and say, "Nobody in their right mind loses money five years in a row and expects to suddenly make money the next year." This is the "Five-Year Rule" in a nutshell. Want the full story? Here's some light reading from the IRS: http://www.irs.gov/pub/irs-pdf/p535.pdf.

Recharacterization as a hobby means one significant change to your financial landscape: your losses will no longer be deductible. So . . . if you make a profit, there is very little difference. But if you lose money in a year (your expenses were larger than your income), you will *not* be able to offset the loss against your income. Let's look at that same example from before and see what kind of impact that would make:

Income	7 Wages, salaries, tips, etc. Attach Form(s) W-2	7	7,051.
	8a **Taxable** interest. Attach Schedule B if required	8a	
Attach Form(s) W-2 here. Also attach Forms W-2G and 1099-R if tax was withheld.	b **Tax-exempt** interest. Do not include on line 8a	8b	
	9a Ordinary dividends. Attach Schedule B if required	9a	
	b Qualified dividends.	9b	
	10 Taxable refunds, credits, or offsets of state and local income taxes	10	0.
If you did not get a W-2, see instructions.	11 Alimony received.	11	
	12 Business income or (loss). Attach Schedule C or C-EZ	12	0.
	13 Capital gain or (loss). Att Sch D if reqd. If not reqd, ck here	13	
	14 Other gains or (losses). Attach Form 4797	14	
	15a IRA distributions	15a	b Taxable amount	15b	19,000.
	16a Pensions and annuities	16a	b Taxable amount	16b	
Enclose, but do not attach, any payment. Also, please use Form 1040-V.	17 Rental real estate, royalties, partnerships, S corporations, trusts, etc. Attach Schedule E	17	
	18 Farm income or (loss). Attach Schedule F	18	
	19 Unemployment compensation	19	14,034.
	20a Social security benefits	20a	b Taxable amount	20b	
	21 Other income	21	
	22 Combine the amounts in the far right column for lines 7 through 21. This is your **total income**	22	40,085.

Figure 1-2

Quite a substantial jump in overall income. In order to avoid characterization as a hobby, the goal is to stay in "business" mode, and the simplest way to do that is to show a profit. Not necessarily every year. One of the many wonderful things about a career as a creative professional is that you are able to do what you love for a living. That's worth a lot to most people. And it's why many artists are "okay" with not making money from their art work. But if you are able to show a profit on paper at least once every five years, it will go a long way to keeping you on track to be considered a business in the eyes of the IRS. You can be converted to hobby status for several other reasons, but none are quite as automatic as the Five-Year Rule, so since it's something you can manage, it's best to mitigate that risk.

Other factors that will help you stay looking "businesslike" in the eyes of the IRS are more qualitative in nature. Here are a few worth considering:

- **Keeping Good Records:** This sounds like a no-brainer, but it makes a lot of sense. How well have you ever kept track of a hobby activity? The amount you've spent on basketball shoes? Or trains? Or vinyl records? But a business—a business needs to know how much money it made and from which sources, what it spent the money on, and ultimately, how much it profited. The better your records, the more serious you appear about your business.

- **Separating Your Funds:** Keeping separate bank accounts is not a necessity—at least, not for self-employed or freelance artists. Once you set up any kind of partnership, LLC, S-corp, or other entity, it will definitely be a part of your life. However, even as a sole proprietor, you have many good reasons to keep your creative activity in a separate bank account. Not only does it reflect well on you looking like a legitimate business in the eyes of the government, it will also limit their scope of inquiry. If your funds are commingled and they have questions about travel expenses, suddenly you've opened up the doors to your entire banking history for the year. Keep the IRS out of your personal account by ensuring them that all your business transactions are in one place. Besides, it will be easier to sort everything out for taxes if it's all in the same place!

- **Putting in the Time:** If it appears as though your business takes up the bare minimum of your attention, it won't look like too viable an activity to the government. If the IRS is looking for you to demonstrate the ability to make a profit, it would help to be able to demonstrate your efforts to grow, to improve, to expand, to work as hard as you can.

CONTRACTORS AND EMPLOYEES

Much confusion exists about the differences between independent contractors and employees. Who gets to decide which you are? Or what the people *you* contract are? It's worth taking a few minutes here to set the story straight so you can avoid pitfalls yourself, as well as update and inform those around you about the truth of the situation. Here are the highlights, in question and answer form for your reading pleasure.

- **Question:** Who gets to decide if someone is an independent contractor or an employee?
  Answer: Nobody does. The relationship decides for itself. In other words, you can't tell anyone that he will be an independent contractor or that she will be an employee and then contradict those words with your actions. The manner in which the two parties interact is the single most important factor in determining independent contractor or employee status.
- **Question:** What's the benefit of being an independent contractor instead of an employee?
  Answer: There's not much of a benefit, not to the "worker" anyway. The main benefit comes to the "employer" in the form of lower payroll taxes. This is why: as an employee, your employer is responsible for matching every dollar of social security and Medicare taxes withheld from your paychecks. The employer then remits his or her half along with your half to the government. For an independent contractor, the would-be employer pays *no half* of taxes, and instead shifts that burden on to the contractor.
- **Question:** So how do you "act" to effect an independent contractor relationship?
  Answer: The best way to think of it is a like a scale that has about eighteen different weights you can place on one side or the other. On the one side, you have "Looks more like an employee," and on the other side, you have "Looks more like an independent

Figure 1-3

contractor." Each of these weights represents a question that will either tip the scale toward one side or another. For example, one question is whether the person in question engages in the work he or she does for you for other people as well. If he or she is not only working for you, but is in the "business" of providing the same service to many people, then that would drop a weight on the "independent contractor" side of the scale. If the person is only working for you, then it would land on the "employee" side of the scale. A full list of the factors to consider can be found here: http://1.usa.gov/JHNYQo.

- **Question:** But what if there's a contract that specifically says the relationship is as an independent contractor?
  Answer: The contract is only one of those weights for the scale. It's always good to have—and if you are about to hire someone and you want them to be viewed and treated as a contractor, it's highly recommended. Again, however, you can't just write down one thing and then act differently. The actions will always speak louder than the words.

- **Question:** What if I was hired as a contractor but treated a lot more like an employee?
  Answer: Sadly this isn't too uncommon. It's happened more frequently since businesses fell on tough times during the recession and were looking to cut costs. And it's *always* been more prevalent in the arts communities for a number of reasons: artists just needing the money and not caring, not knowing any better, nonprofits on tight budgets . . . Whatever the reason, you don't have to stand for it. If you find yourself staring at a big form 1099-MISC at the end of the year that causes your tax bill to reach astronomical proportions *and* you are confident that you are really an employee in contractor clothing, there is relief for you. You can notify the IRS, and they will review the situation. If they agree with the determination, the employer will be responsible for its share of the payroll taxes and you will feel at least a little relief.

CASE STUDY

I had a client who had been doing grant writing for a nonprofit for five years when he came into my office for some tax help. He had been slammed with incredibly high self-employment taxes because this was his main source of income. In fact, he only did this work for them. He worked in their offices on their computers on a set schedule that the nonprofit determined. He was given detailed instructions about how to carry out his job. Yet despite all these factors, they were still trying to pay him as an independent contractor. When we reviewed the situation, he felt this treatment was unfair and wanted the IRS to review the matter. They looked into it and determined that he was in fact functioning in the capacity of an employee and not a contractor. The IRS issued the nonprofit a bill for five years of back-taxes on his wages plus interest and penalties. My client received a refund for the employer portion of payroll taxes that he shouldn't have been paying. I think there's a lesson here for both businesses and the people they hire. If you're trying to pay people as contractors because it can save you a few bucks here and there, it's usually not worth it, because the risk of getting caught is too great. And if you are unfairly being treated as a contractor when you should be an employee, raise the issue. Even if you're not interested in getting the organization in trouble, you could at least argue for proper treatment going forward.

Study Questions

1. Can you still consider yourself a business if you are losing money in a year—that is, if your income is less than your expenses?

2. What happens to your acting, music, or other creative activity if you show losses for five years in a row? How does that impact your taxes?

3. What three things can you do to further solidify your stance that you are a business in the eyes of the IRS?

4. Which is more beneficial *to the payer of the money*: paying someone as an independent contractor or as an employee?

Answers

1. Yes, you can treat yourself as a business even if you have *no* income in a year (though not indefinitely).

2. After five straight years of losses, the IRS recharacterizes you as a hobby. This means that on your tax return, you will no longer be able to deduct the losses from your creative pursuit against money you make elsewhere.

3. Keep good records, separate your business and personal funds, and put in the time to show you are seriously pursuing a career in the field.

4. The payer benefits more from paying someone as an independent contractor. Specifically, they are avoiding having to contribute half of your payroll taxes.

2

Being Self-Employed

HOW PEOPLE PAY YOU

If you find yourself characterized as any of the following, this chapter is for you: freelance, self-employed, independent contractor, solopreneur, sole proprietor. These words all mean essentially the same thing: you are a one-person business unto yourself—not incorporated or legally existing in any other way. Your name is your own name (usually), the tax ID number that you file the activity under is your own social security number (again, usually). Even if you are not currently self-employed, it would be a good idea to read through this chapter for two reasons. First, most creative professionals and artists will be self-employed at *some point* in their lives. Second, it will help you to understand some of the juxtapositions I will create in subsequent chapters.

Enough of a preamble. Self-employment is the "default" form of business for an artist or creative. Why? Well it doesn't take anything to get started. You simply hold yourself out for hire and . . . *bam!* You're self-

Figure 2-1

employed. There was no paperwork to file, no government fees. So when people pay you for services rendered, you're going to collect money without any taxes withheld. While this may sound amazing at first glance, playing this chess game out will show that you are still going to be responsible for paying the taxes you used to pay as an employee. More taxes, in fact, if you aren't careful about managing your income and expenses. What does this income look like? For the gigging musician, it could be a session fee from a band leader. For an actor, a stipend for rehearsing and performing in a show. For a sculptor, it could be a grant received to create a work.

Key Point

N.B. Be careful of "grants" and other such sources of income. While they sound like they should not be taxable income (especially since they often come from nonprofit organizations), they are in fact subject to both income tax and self-employment tax. You will be able to deduct agvainst that income all related expenses, but to the extent that you pocket any of that money, you will pay taxes on it.

How do you know when you're about to receive money and not have taxes withheld? Being presented with an "independent contractor agreement" is a good hint. If someone is asking you to sign one of these contracts, it usually means that they are intending to pay you as a self-employed individual and are therefore intending not to *withhold* any taxes out of your pay. There could be many reasons for this, but just be sure that the reality of your working relationship reflects the decision to be paid as an independent contractor versus an employee. Another good tip-off that you're about to receive pay without taxes being withheld is being asked to fill out a W9. The form W9 simply asks you to verify your name, address, and social security number (see fig. 2-2). It is the very same information that the person paying you will ultimately use to file your 1099-MISC at the end of the year. And that 1099-MISC, for those of you who have never received one, is the self-employed equivalent of a W2.

Form W-9
(Rev. December 2011)
Department of the Treasury
Internal Revenue Service

**Request for Taxpayer
Identification Number and Certification**

Give Form to the
requester. Do not
send to the IRS.

Name (as shown on your income tax return)

Business name/disregarded entity name, if different from above

Check appropriate box for federal tax classification:

☐ Individual/sole proprietor   ☐ C Corporation   ☐ S Corporation   ☐ Partnership   ☐ Trust/estate

☐ Limited liability company. Enter the tax classification (C=C corporation, S=S corporation, P=partnership) ▶ ....

☐ Other (see instructions) ▶

☐ Exempt payee

Address (number, street, and apt. or suite no.)

Requester's name and address (optional)

City, state, and ZIP code

List account number(s) here (optional)

Print or type   See Specific Instructions on page 2.

Part I   Taxpayer Identification Number (TIN)

Enter your TIN in the appropriate box. The TIN provided must match the name given on the "Name" line to avoid backup withholding. For individuals, this is your social security number (SSN). However, for a resident alien, sole proprietor, or disregarded entity, see the Part I instructions on page 3. For other entities, it is your employer identification number (EIN). If you do not have a number, see How to get a TIN on page 3.

Note. If the account is in more than one name, see the chart on page 4 for guidelines on whose number to enter.

Social security number

☐☐☐ – ☐☐ – ☐☐☐☐

Employer identification number

☐☐ – ☐☐☐☐☐☐☐

Part II   Certification

Under penalties of perjury, I certify that:

1. The number shown on this form is my correct taxpayer identification number (or I am waiting for a number to be issued to me), and

2. I am not subject to backup withholding because: (a) I am exempt from backup withholding, or (b) I have not been notified by the Internal Revenue Service (IRS) that I am subject to backup withholding as a result of a failure to report all interest or dividends, or (c) the IRS has notified me that I am no longer subject to backup withholding, and

3. I am a U.S. citizen or other U.S. person (defined below).

Certification instructions. You must cross out item 2 above if you have been notified by the IRS that you are currently subject to backup withholding because you have failed to report all interest and dividends on your tax return. For real estate transactions, item 2 does not apply. For mortgage interest paid, acquisition or abandonment of secured property, cancellation of debt, contributions to an individual retirement arrangement (IRA), and generally, payments other than interest and dividends, you are not required to sign the certification, but you must provide your correct TIN. See the instructions on page 4.

Sign Here   Signature of U.S. person ▶   Date ▶

General Instructions

Section references are to the Internal Revenue Code unless otherwise noted.

Purpose of Form

A person who is required to file an information return with the IRS must obtain your correct taxpayer identification number (TIN) to report, for example, income paid to you, real estate transactions, mortgage interest you paid, acquisition or abandonment of secured property, cancellation of debt, or contributions you made to an IRA.

Use Form W-9 only if you are a U.S. person (including a resident alien), to provide your correct TIN to the person requesting it (the requester) and, when applicable, to:

1. Certify that the TIN you are giving is correct (or you are waiting for a number to be issued),

2. Certify that you are not subject to backup withholding, or

3. Claim exemption from backup withholding if you are a U.S. exempt payee. If applicable, you are also certifying that as a U.S. person, your allocable share of any partnership income from a U.S. trade or business is not subject to the withholding tax on foreign partners' share of effectively connected income.

Note. If a requester gives you a form other than Form W-9 to request your TIN, you must use the requester's form if it is substantially similar to this Form W-9.

Definition of a U.S. person. For federal tax purposes, you are considered a U.S. person if you are:

• An individual who is a U.S. citizen or U.S. resident alien,

• A partnership, corporation, company, or association created or organized in the United States or under the laws of the United States,

• An estate (other than a foreign estate), or

• A domestic trust (as defined in Regulations section 301.7701-7).

Special rules for partnerships. Partnerships that conduct a trade or business in the United States are generally required to pay a withholding tax on any foreign partners' share of income from such business. Further, in certain cases where a Form W-9 has not been received, a partnership is required to presume that a partner is a foreign person, and pay the withholding tax. Therefore, if you are a U.S. person that is a partner in a partnership conducting a trade or business in the United States, provide Form W-9 to the partnership to establish your U.S. status and avoid withholding on your share of partnership income.

Cat. No. 10231X   Form **W-9** (Rev. 12-2011)

Figure 2-2

And then what? Are you going to deposit this money in your personal checking account and move on? Ideally, no. If at all possible, I want you to deposit this money into a separate account that only has money coming from your self-employed creative endeavor. It's a great way to help you keep track of the untaxed income you're racking up during the year.

And from that point on, you'll be able to easily see how much of that money needs to be set aside for the government.

HOW YOU REPORT YOUR INCOME

That 1099-MISC form from the individual or company that paid you will be your key method of verifying the amount of income you received in the previous calendar year. Where does all this income get reported? On Schedule C of your individual income tax return (see fig. 2-3). If you are used to filing a 1040EZ with just your W2 wages and tax withholdings, you're about to enter a whole new world of filing taxes. But not to fear—I am going to arm you with enough understanding to know how it all works and when it's appropriate to turn it over to professional hands. The Schedule C is where any self-employed activity could get reported, and this is where your photography studio, freelance editing, or modeling income will land.

Should you take the amounts listed on your Form(s) 1099-MISC at face value? You *could*. You certainly could. After all, the 1099 (like a W2) is reported to the government. It's the official number. Just like a W2 would be. So if you didn't argue with what the 1099 said, nobody would ever bring it up and question you. Why then give it a second look? One would hope that all organizations are equally proficient in managing their finances/numbers/tax filings. However (and this is particularly the case in arts and creative organizations), all are not created equal. This is to say, if your band manager has a hard time getting everyone their show dates, or the company manager has a hard time getting actors their paychecks on time, or the magazine you're writing for confuses assignments regularly, they may be the kind of group more likely to make an error in reporting your income.

So what do you do? Track it. Track all of them. Even the ones you think have their act together. Although the disorganized are *more* likely to make a mistake, it can happen to anyone. And if you report too much income on your tax return, nobody will be there to catch you or stop you from paying too much in taxes. Life as a practicing artist is difficult enough. Don't make it any harder on yourself by increasing the amount of taxes you have to pay on your income.

What other kind of income needs to be reported on this Schedule C? Well, the 1099-MISC forms will come from any individual or organization

SCHEDULE C (Form 1040) Department of the Treasury Internal Revenue Service (99)	**Profit or Loss From Business** (Sole Proprietorship) ▶ For information on Schedule C and its instructions, go to *www.irs.gov/schedulec* ▶ Attach to Form 1040, 1040NR, or 1041; partnerships generally must file Form 1065.		OMB No. 1545-0074 2011 Attachment Sequence No. 09

Name of proprietor — Social security number (SSN)

A	Principal business or profession, including product or service (see instructions)	B Enter code from instructions ▶
C	Business name. If no separate business name, leave blank.	D Employer ID number (EIN), (see instr.)

E Business address (including suite or room no.) ▶
City, town or post office, state, and ZIP code

F Accounting method: (1) ☐ Cash (2) ☐ Accrual (3) ☐ Other (specify) ▶
G Did you "materially participate" in the operation of this business during 2011? If "No," see instructions for limit on losses . ☐ Yes ☐ No
H If you started or acquired this business during 2011, check here . . . . ▶ ☐
I Did you make any payments in 2011 that would require you to file Form(s) 1099? (see instructions) . . . . . . ☐ Yes ☐ No
J If "Yes," did you or will you file all required Forms 1099? . . . . ☐ Yes ☐ No

Part I Income

1a	Merchant card and third party payments. For 2011, enter -0-	1a			
b	Gross receipts or sales not entered on line 1a (see instructions) . .	1b			
c	Income reported to you on Form W-2 if the "Statutory Employee" box on that form was checked. **Caution.** See instr. before completing this line	1c			
d	**Total gross receipts.** Add lines 1a through 1c			1d	
2	Returns and allowances plus any other adjustments (see instructions)			2	
3	Subtract line 2 from line 1d			3	
4	Cost of goods sold (from line 42)			4	
5	**Gross profit.** Subtract line 4 from line 3			5	
6	Other income, including federal and state gasoline or fuel tax credit or refund (see instructions)			6	
7	**Gross income.** Add lines 5 and 6 . . . . ▶			7	

Part II Expenses Enter expenses for business use of your home only on line 30.

8	Advertising	8			18	Office expense (see instructions)	18	
9	Car and truck expenses (see instructions).	9			19	Pension and profit-sharing plans .	19	
					20	Rent or lease (see instructions):		
10	Commissions and fees .	10			a	Vehicles, machinery, and equipment	20a	
11	Contract labor (see instructions)	11			b	Other business property . . .	20b	
12	Depletion	12			21	Repairs and maintenance . . .	21	
13	Depreciation and section 179 expense deduction (not included in Part III) (see instructions). . . .	13			22	Supplies (not included in Part III) .	22	
					23	Taxes and licenses	23	
					24	Travel, meals, and entertainment:		
14	Employee benefit programs (other than on line 19). .	14			a	Travel	24a	
15	Insurance (other than health)	15			b	Deductible meals and entertainment (see instructions) .	24b	
16	Interest:				25	Utilities	25	
a	Mortgage (paid to banks, etc.)	16a			26	Wages (less employment credits) .	26	
b	Other	16b			27a	Other expenses (from line 48) . .	27a	
17	Legal and professional services	17			b	**Reserved for future use** . . .	27b	

28	**Total expenses** before expenses for business use of home. Add lines 8 through 27a . . . . . . ▶	28	
29	Tentative profit or (loss). Subtract line 28 from line 7	29	
30	Expenses for business use of your home. Attach **Form 8829.** Do **not** report such expenses elsewhere . .	30	
31	**Net profit or (loss).** Subtract line 30 from line 29. • If a profit, enter on both **Form 1040, line 12** (or **Form 1040NR, line 13**) and on **Schedule SE, line 2.** If you entered an amount on line 1c, see instr. Estates and trusts, enter on **Form 1041, line 3.** • If a loss, you **must** go to line 32.	31	
32	If you have a loss, check the box that describes your investment in this activity (see instructions). • If you checked 32a, enter the loss on both **Form 1040, line 12,** (or **Form 1040NR, line 13**) and on **Schedule SE, line 2.** If you entered an amount on line 1c, see the instructions for line 31. Estates and trusts, enter on **Form 1041, line 3.** • If you checked 32b, you **must** attach **Form 6198.** Your loss may be limited.	32a ☐ All investment is at risk. 32b ☐ Some investment is not at risk.

For Paperwork Reduction Act Notice, see your tax return instructions. Cat. No. 11334P Schedule C (Form 1040) 2011

Figure 2-3

that paid you more than $600 in a calendar year. There could be plenty of people that also paid you as a self-employed individual, but simply paid you less than that much in a year. Does that mean you don't need to include that income? I wouldn't skip it . . . and here's why. *If* you ever get pulled for an audit (and that's a *big* "if" since only 1 percent of all individual returns get pulled for an audit),[*] there's a very easy test they will do on your income. They will ask for your twelve monthly bank statements, total up your deposits for each month, and compare it to the income you reported. If your deposits are more than the income reported, you'll be asked to explain why. If the reason is you received a large gift from your great-aunt, you could be in the clear. If, however, the reason is you *only* reported income that was on 1099s and skipped the rest, you'll have to go back and pay not only the taxes related, but interest and penalties as well. Here's an example of how that might play out if you get busted three years later:

	Reported Originally	Reported 3 Years Later
Income from 1099s	22500	22500
Other Self-Employed Income	0	8800
Self-Employed Deductions	10250	10250
Taxable Income	12250	21050
Total Taxes	3675	6315
Interest	0	758
Penalties	0	1137
Total Due	3675	8210

Figure 2-4

While I'm on the subject of reporting your income, there are a few self-employed creative professions (barbers, stylists, personal shoppers, aestheticians, buskers, to name a few) who deal with tips more than others. This is not to mention the stereotypical "second job" of any creative pro: waiting tables or tending bar. Tips are sometimes reported on your W2, and if they are, then this issue does not apply to you. On the other hand, if your tips are not reported, you are responsible for tracking them and reporting them on your own. Why? For the same reason you want to report "non-1099" income. It's going to show up in your bank statement; you'll have to explain it someday. You might as well explain it and deal with it in the moment.

N.B. Anyone who tries to tell you that there is a magic percentage of your tips that you can/should report is making it up. The only percentage of your tips that is okay to report is 100 percent. Anything short of that, and you are making a choice to take your chances of getting busted. The choice is yours, but just know that no auditor will accept reporting anything shy of 100 percent.

---

[*] *Internal Revenue Service Data Book, 2010*, Publication 55B (Washington, DC: IRS, March 2011).

HOW YOU REPORT YOUR EXPENSES

Reporting your expenses will happen as a part of completing the same schedule as your self-employed income. Schedule C of your individual tax return will include not only the income from Forms 1099-MISC (and any other self-employed income you may have) but also all deductible expenses. I'll go through which kinds of expenses are applicable in a later chapter, and I'll also talk about the right system to use to track them. For the time being, let's assume that you know the things to keep track of and you have good records supporting your spending all year.

The expenses for your creative business may or may not "fit in" well with the categories listed on Schedule C. Don't worry if you find yourself trying to fit a square peg into a round hole. The categories listed on Schedule C are meant to be broadly applicable to *all kinds of businesses* and rarely are sufficient to describe all the kinds of things that are deductible for self-employed creatives. But is there any kind of translation possible? Sure. You don't have to give up entirely and call everything "other." Here's an example of a few categories listed on Schedule C and how they may manifest in your business:

How it's listed on Schedule C:	But for someone working as a:	It may actually be your:
Advertising	Model	Comp cards
Contract Labor	Photographer	Models
Legal and Professional	Author	Tax Prep Fees from last year
Rent or lease	Filmmaker	Camera or light rentals
Repairs and maintenance	Guitarist	Tubes for your amplifier
Supplies	Anything	This is a good catchall…
Taxes and licenses	Barber	Your annual state licensure fee
Travel	Band	Tour expenses (but not people-related)
Meals and entertainment	Literary Agent	Dinners and drinks with prospective clients
Utilities	Graphic Designer	Internet connection at home (if you work from home)

Figure 2-5

Of course, when you have to list all those other deductions that don't fit any of these other categories, there is always the "other" section. You'll further break these expenses down on the last page of Schedule C (and attach additional pages if needed). Here is where you can include things like makeup, coaching sessions, contest submission fees, and anything else that you spent money on in pursuit of your artistic career.

How do these deductions impact your return? Well they're going to offset that self-employed income I talked about in the last section. You're ultimately going to drive down to a "net profit (or loss) from self-employment." That figure (your income minus your expenses) is what will land on the first page of your 1040 individual tax return (see fig. 2-6).

SCHEDULE C (Form 1040)		**Profit or Loss From Business** (Sole Proprietorship)		OMB No. 1545-0074
Department of the Treasury Internal Revenue Service (99)		► For information on Schedule C and its instructions, go to *www.irs.gov/schedulec*. ►Attach to Form 1040, 1040NR, or 1041; partnerships generally must file Form 1065.		**2011** Attachment Sequence No. **09**

Name of proprietor | | Social security number (SSN)

A Principal business or profession, including product or service (see instructions)   ACTOR | **B** Enter code from instructions ► 711510

C Business name. If no separate business name, leave blank. | **D** Employer ID number (EIN), (see instrs)

E Business address (including suite or room no.) ►
City, town or post office, state, and ZIP code

F Accounting method: (1) ☒ Cash (2) ☐ Accrual (3) ☐ Other (specify) ►

G Did you 'materially participate' in the operation of this business during 2011? If 'No,' see instructions for limit on losses . . . . . ☒ Yes ☐ No

H If you started or acquired this business during 2011, check here . . . . ►☐

I Did you make any payments in 2011 that would require you to file Form(s) 1099? (see instructions) . . . . ☐ Yes ☒ No

J If 'Yes,' did you or will you file all required Forms 1099? . . . . ☐ Yes ☐ No

Part I Income

1 a Merchant card and third party payments. For 2011, enter -0-	**1a**	0.	
b Gross receipts or sales not entered on line 1a (see instructions)	**1b**	14,105.	
c Income reported to you on Form W-2 if the 'Statutory Employee' box on that form was checked. **Caution.** See instructions before completing this line	**1c**		
d Total gross receipts. Add lines 1a through 1c	**1d**		14,105.
2 Returns and allowances plus any other adjustments (see instructions)	**2**		
3 Subtract line 2 from line 1d	**3**		14,105.
4 Cost of goods sold (from line 42)	**4**		
5 **Gross profit.** Subtract line 4 from line 3	**5**		14,105.
6 Other income, including federal and state gasoline or fuel tax credit or refund (see instructions)	**6**		
7 **Gross income.** Add lines 5 and 6 . . . . ►	**7**		14,105.

Part II Expenses. Enter expenses for business use of your home only on line 30.

8 Advertising	**8**		**18** Office expense (see instructions)	**18**		94.
9 Car and truck expenses (see instructions)	**9**	351.	**19** Pension and profit-sharing plans	**19**		
10 Commissions and fees	**10**	3,631.	**20** Rent or lease (see instructions):			
11 Contract labor (see instructions)	**11**		**a** Vehicles, machinery, and equipment	**20a**		
12 Depletion	**12**		**b** Other business property	**20b**		
13 Depreciation and section 179 expense deduction (not included in Part III) (see instructions)	**13**	647.	**21** Repairs and maintenance	**21**		
			22 Supplies (not included in Part III)	**22**		
			23 Taxes and licenses	**23**		
			24 Travel, meals, and entertainment:			
14 Employee benefit programs (other than on line 19)	**14**		**a** Travel	**24a**		1,075.
15 Insurance (other than health) . .	**15**		**b** Deductible meals and entertainment (see instructions)	**24b**		22.
16 Interest:			**25** Utilities	**25**		
a Mortgage (paid to banks, etc) . .	**16a**		**26** Wages (less employment credits)	**26**		
b Other	**16b**		**27a** Other expenses (from line 48)	**27a**		-3,344.
17 Legal & professional services . .	**17**	275.	**b** Reserved for future use	**27b**		
28 **Total expenses** before expenses for business use of home. Add lines 8 through 27a . . . . ►				**28**		2,751.
29 Tentative profit or (loss). Subtract line 28 from line 7				**29**		11,354.
30 Expenses for business use of your home. Attach Form 8829. Do **not** report such expenses elsewhere				**30**		3,998.
31 **Net profit or (loss).** Subtract line 30 from line 29.						

• If a profit, enter on both **Form 1040, line 12** (or **Form 1040NR, line 13**) and on **Schedule SE, line 2.** If you entered an amount on line 1c, see instructions. Estates and trusts, enter on **Form 1041, line 3.** | | | | **31** | | 7,356.

• If a loss, you **must** go to line 32.

32 If you have a loss, check the box that describes your investment in this activity (see instructions).

• If you checked 32a, enter the loss on both **Form 1040, line 12,** (or **Form 1040NR, line 13**) and on **Schedule SE, line 2.** If you entered an amount on line 1c, see the instructions for line 31. Estates and trusts, enter on **Form 1041, line 3.** | **32a** ☐ All investment is at risk.

• If you checked 32b, you **must** attach **Form 6198.** Your loss may be limited. | **32b** ☐ Some investment is not at risk.

BAA For Paperwork Reduction Act Notice, see your tax return instructions. | Schedule C (Form 1040) 2011

FDIZ0112 10/25/11

	d Total number of exemptions claimed		above . . . ►	2.
Income	**7** Wages, salaries, tips, etc. Attach Form(s) W-2	**7**		63,927.
	8a Taxable interest. Attach Schedule B if required	**8a**		98.
	b Tax-exempt interest. **Do not** include on line 8a	**8b**			
Attach Form(s) W-2 here. Also attach Forms W-2G and 1099-R if tax was withheld.	**9a** Ordinary dividends. Attach Schedule B if required	**9a**		
	b Qualified dividends	**9b**			
	10 Taxable refunds, credits, or offsets of state and local income taxes	**10**		0.
	11 Alimony received	**11**		
If you did not get a W-2, see instructions.	**12** Business income or (loss). Attach Schedule C or C-EZ	**12**	>	7,356.
	13 Capital gain or (loss). Att Sch D if reqd. If not reqd, ck here . . . . ►☐	**13**		
	14 Other gains or (losses). Attach Form 4797	**14**		
	15a IRA distributions	**15a**		**b** Taxable amount	**15b**	
	16a Pensions and annuities . . .	**16a**		**b** Taxable amount	**16b**	
	17 Rental real estate, royalties, partnerships, S corporations, trusts, etc. Attach Schedule E	**17**		
Enclose, but do not attach, any payment. Also, please use Form 1040-V.	**18** Farm income or (loss). Attach Schedule F	**18**		
	19 Unemployment compensation	**19**		
	20a Social security benefits	**20a**		**b** Taxable amount	**20b**	
	21 Other income	**21**		
	22 Combine the amounts in the far right column for lines 7 through 21. This is your **total income** . . . . ►	**22**		71,381.

Figure 2-6

And when that number transfers to your 1040, that's where you'll figure out the amount of income tax and self-employment tax due. If a home-office deduction makes sense for you—that is, if you have a work space that's used regularly and exclusively for your creative business—then be sure to include that as the final deduction before calculating your net profit from self-employment. There's a separate schedule for the home office (Form 8829), but I won't go into too much detail on how to fill it out. Remember, we're here for the big picture.

ADVANTAGES TO STAYING SELF-EMPLOYED

There are several advantages to staying self-employed, and it can be a successful strategy for you for years to come. Fans of the KISS (Keep it Simple, Stupid) philosophy will appreciate this logic. For starters, there is very little you need to do to get started as a self-employed activity. When you go out into the world and say "I'm open for business," you've essentially completed all the necessary steps to being a sole proprietor. Now, you may want to involve a few of the other self-employed "add-ons" mentioned later in this section, but at a minimum, you're ready for action.

Being self-employed in this fashion means you can go out and earn money in any number of ways: making and selling things, recording and licensing things, or offering your time and services for sale. Your business name is your name. Your business address is your address. Your business tax identification number for the IRS will be your social security number. There are no forms to file with the state, no fees to pay, no additional tax returns you'll need to file. Everything will remain on your individual tax return (Form 1040) on a Schedule C. Simple indeed.

Aside from an obvious lack of paperwork requirements, the other primary benefit of staying self-employed as a sole proprietor comes in years when you are losing money. Now, it's never ideal to be spending more on your business than it generates for you in income. However, the reality of getting a business started is that you have good years and slow years. And it's rather common for a business to lose some money in the first year of operations. There is often an up-front investment in legal fees, supplies, advertising, and so forth that may amount to more than you are able to generate in year one. Or even year two. If you recall the conversation about the "Five-Year Rule," you'd theoretically

Figure 2-7

be able to lose money for five years before the IRS ever wrote you a letter indicating they now consider this to be a "hobby" and not a "business." And what benefit do sole proprietors have in years when they lose money? In the world of tax planning, there's an axiom (that I'm sure *I* didn't come up with, but somebody at some point did) that says you try to keep your losses close to you and your gains far away.

This principle makes good sense. In years when you lose money, whether it's from your business or from sale of investments, you want to recognize as much of that loss as possible and be able to offset that loss against money you make anywhere else in your life. That's exactly how this works for sole proprietors. Some other "pass-through" forms of incorporating also carry the ability to recognize your losses, but there's nothing that comes as close to your individual return as showing it right there on Schedule C of your individual taxes.

Even as you start making a profit, filing this activity on Schedule C can be an inexpensive, easy way to deal with your new business. And it can grow with you as you grow. Even as a sole proprietor, you will be able to "add on" several features to your business:

- You could register for a separate business tax identification number (a.k.a. tax ID or EIN) which will allow you to isolate the income and expenses of your business to a unique government ID distinct from your social security number.
- With a separate tax ID, you could also go and get a separate bank account for your business. This can be very helpful for a number of reasons. For starters, when you get a little behind in tracking your income and expenses (and let's be honest, it's going to happen

to everyone), you need only to look through your one set of bank statements and you'll know right away that every transaction in there *must be* classified somehow as a business expense or income. Not only that, if you happen to be one of the lucky few who has your return reviewed, you will only have to turn over *that one set* of bank statements and not your personal account as well— since there was no business activity in that other account, right? Limiting the scope of the government snooping around in your affairs is always a good idea.

• You can use your new tax ID to hire employees as well. Sure, from day one you can bring in *other independent contractors* to work for you, paying them much in the same way that you get paid, but if you want to hire employees and withhold taxes for them, provide benefits, and so forth, you'll need that separate tax ID for your business.

• You can even set up retirement accounts and have operations in many states as a sole proprietor.

You may be wondering at what point you would ever decide *not* to be a sole proprietor . . . Well, the answer has a lot to do with this thing called "self-employment tax" and the awfully large bite it can take out of your profits if you start realizing a decent level of success with your business. To see if this may be a concern for you, read on through the coming chapters about incorporating as a distinct and totally separate business. But hopefully this chapter has given you a good understanding of what it means to operate as a sole proprietor and the primary benefits to running your business in this fashion.

THE SELF-EMPLOYED CALENDAR OF IMPORTANT DATES

Here are some dates you may want to add to your calendar to help you keep tabs on your obligations. Your advisors may give you a few additional dates to remember beyond these, but for a one-person, self-employed operation, these should be the majority of the events during the year. All dates are consistent year to year, except when they fall on weekends or holidays. In those cases, just push the deadline forward to the next business day.

- **JANUARY**
  - **15: Individual Estimated Tax Payment #4:** This is the final installment of your prior year's estimated tax payments. (Remember, these payments apply to cases where you accumulate over $1,000 in tax liability over the course of the year.)
  - **31: 1099 and W2 Deadline #1:** This is the deadline to provide W2s to your employees and 1099s to your independent contractors. There is a separate deadline (to follow) for furnishing these forms to the IRS, which will allow you to correct any mistakes employees bring up.
- **FEBRUARY**
  - **28: 1099 and W2 Deadline #2:** One month after needing to send W2s and 1099s to your employees and contractors, you will now have to send in the final copies to the IRS and Social Security Administration. Don't forget W3s and 1096s—these are the "cover sheets" that accompany W2s and 1099s and let the government know how many forms to expect.
- **MARCH (none)**
- **APRIL**
  - **15: Individual Income Tax Return:** This is the due date for your individual return (Form 1040) or the extension (Form 4868). Remember that extending your return buys you an extra six months to file but not to pay, so if you have a balance due, you may want to get an estimate of your payment on file at this point even if you don't complete the return. Not doing so creates interest from this date until you pay.
  - **15: Individual Estimated Tax Payment #1:** This is your first payment toward your current-year tax liability.
- **MAY (none)**
- **JUNE**
  - **15: Individual Estimated Tax Payment #2:**

This is your second payment toward your current-year tax liability.

• **JULY (none)**
• **AUGUST (none)**
• **SEPTEMBER**
  ○ **15: Individual Estimated Tax Payment #3:** This is your third payment toward your current-year tax liability.
• **OCTOBER**
  ○ **15: Individual Income Tax Return Extension Deadline:** If you filed an extension in April of this year, your individual tax return is due six months later, on October 15.
• **NOVEMBER (none)**
• **DECEMBER (none)**

As you can see, the requirements are fairly light for a self-employed individual, especially those that don't have estimated payments to make. Remember that these are just the IRS requirements. Your advisors may want to schedule additional check-ins or follow-up points that would be great additions to your calendar of important business dates. And if you'd like some links to automatically add these dates to your calendar system, click here: http://www.rockstarcpa.com/minding-your-business.

LET'S MAP IT OUT (INCOME, EXPENSES, AND TAXES)

So what does the big picture look like when you're self-employed? See figure 2-8 for an example of the ins and outs, the systems that will take care of your business so you can do what you love.

What does this scary mess of blocks and arrows mean? Let's break it down simply.

Initially, you go through the year collecting bits and pieces of source material. Just like collecting and saving riffs that inspire you musically or short bits of dialogue you will later string together into a novel, these bits of income and expenses are the source of your financial picture for the year. The income gets tracked in a system such as Outright or in your spreadsheet, and later will be verified by the 1099s you receive. The expenses (wherever they come from) also get tracked in Outright or your spreadsheet. The physical paper created along the way gets saved in a folder or gets scanned up by a smartphone app or to your computer. And to bring it all together into a tax return, you take the income reported on 1099s, deductions tracked in your spreadsheet, and any estimated payments you've deposited along the way, and report it all on your individual tax return.

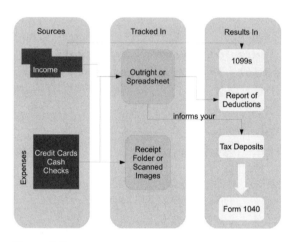

Figure 2-8

Study Questions

1. Do you have to set aside money for taxes when you're paid as an independent contractor? What about as an employee?
2. At what dollar amount are vendors required to provide you a 1099? What do you do about those who pay you less than that amount?
3. On what tax form do self-employed income and expenses get reported?
4. What is the most frequently utilized sole proprietor add-on?
5. What are the differences between the terms *self-employed, sole proprietor, solopreneur, independent contractor,* and *freelancer?*

Answers

1. Yes, the income you earn as an independent contractor does not have any taxes withheld, and accordingly you

need to save the appropriate amount to pay in at the end of the year. As an employee, however, taxes are withheld from each paycheck and sent to the IRS on your behalf.

2. Payers are required to issue you a 1099 if you receive over $600 *in the calendar year* for services you perform. Reimbursements don't count in this total. If you receive less than $600 in the year from a given person, you won't get a tax form, but the income is still reportable on your tax return.

3. Income and expenses of self-employed individuals is reported on Schedule C of your individual tax return (Form 1040).

4. The most frequent addition to a typical self-employed setup is to add a separate tax ID number that distinguishes the activity from yourself, and allows you to use your social security number less frequently.

5. Nothing. These are all terms that refer to one person engaging in a for-profit activity, not as an employee, and without establishing a separate business outside him- or herself.

3

Forming a Separate Business

THE DIFFERENT FLAVORS

If you start considering setting up a separate business entity for your-self, it's important to know the different flavors of business out there. The three I will review in detail are C-corporations, S-corporations, and partnerships. Each of them carry their own benefits and drawbacks, additional responsibilities and potential savings. When people you talk to reference "incorporating," they could be speaking of any of these, so it's important to be clear about exactly what is being discussed. To give you a sense of what these are, let's look at a quick definition of each:

- **C-Corporation:** The default setting for any corporation. But most businesses that stay C-corporations (or C-corps) tend to be the biggest of corporations (think GE, Motorola, Boeing, etc.).
- **S-Corporation:** Though it really stands for "Subchapter S of the Internal Revenue Code," you can think of S-corporations (or S-corps) as small business corporations. They have tax treatment that benefits most smaller businesses.
- **Partnership:** Can be loosely formed by the association of more than one person engaged in the same activity or more concretely established by setting up an LLC. I'll discuss partnerships and LLCs later in this section.

C-CORPORATION

Let's begin with a C-corporation. The process of setting up a C-corp is fairly simple, despite the fact that they are typically used for the largest of companies in the world. In order to establish a C-corp, you need only do the following:

1. File articles of incorporation in the state in which you are operating.
2. Fill out the online application with the IRS to obtain a new tax ID number (EIN) for your business.

That is essentially all that's required. And typically you can do this for under a couple hundred dollars. But the reason that C-corps are so seldom used by artists and creatives is that it takes a substantial amount of income to justify a C-corp status. Why? Because a C-corp involves the dreaded "double taxation" of corporations. Meaning? Well, let's follow along and see where the taxes come into play:

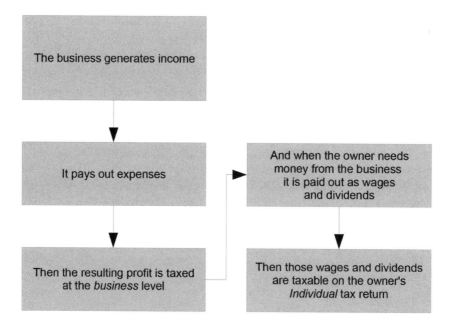

Figure 3-1

Did you see it? The business has to pay its own corporate tax rate (often much higher than individual tax rates), and then the owner has to again pay individual-level taxes on the money that he or she takes for him- or herself. When does this make sense? Only when the tax burden that the business is creating is *so* great that it is overburdensome for the owners to pay for in the given year. (Read: when they make a *lot* of money.)

But corporations are getting away with paying 0 percent tax rates, right? Isn't that what the whole "occupy" movement is about? Yes and no. The corporations that are getting away with incredibly low tax rates are doing so usually for two reasons. First, they are generating *so* much profit that they can afford to bottle some of it up in places they can't get at it. Does this make sense for an enormous global bank or mining company? Sure. But it isn't a very practical strategy for a business owner who needs to support him- or herself with the proceeds of his or her work. In other words, this is a strategy for the big guys. The other thing they are doing is hiring hundreds (yes hundreds) of attorneys who all sit in a room and whose full-time job it is to dissect the tax code and find ways to stretch the laws to their limit. Again, this is probably not the best use of your time or money and is a strategy for the big guys.

So for us 99-percenters, let's assume that a C-corp makes sense only when you become wildly successful, and at that point you will refer back to this chapter and note the two simple steps it will take for you to get started.

S-CORPORATION

S-corps on the other hand are a very commonly used form of business by artists and creatives, especially those who need to set up a business around themselves—a business of one. If you started out as a self-employed creative and reached a point where your self-employment taxes became really excessive, creating an S-corp to pass your income and expenses through is an excellent strategy to reduce your annual tax bill. And they are not too complicated to set up either. What's involved here?

1. File articles of incorporation in the state in which you are operating.
2. Fill out the online application with the IRS to obtain a new tax ID number (EIN) for your business.
3. File an S-corporation election with the IRS to let them know you would like to be treated as an S-corp for tax purposes (Form 2553).

<table>
<tr><td colspan="2">Form **2553**
(Rev. December 2007)
Department of the Treasury
Internal Revenue Service</td><td>**Election by a Small Business Corporation**
(Under section 1362 of the Internal Revenue Code)
▶ See Parts II and III on page 3 and the separate instructions.
▶ The corporation can fax this form to the IRS (see separate instructions).</td></tr>
</table>

Note. This election to be an S corporation can be accepted only if all the tests are met under **Who May Elect** on pag shareholders have signed the consent statement; an officer has signed below; and the exact name and address o required form information are provided.

Part I   Election Information

Type or Print	Name (see instructions)	A Employe
	Number, street, and room or suite no. (If a P.O. box, see instructions.)	B Date incc
	City or town, state, and ZIP code	C State of i

D Check the applicable box(es) if the corporation, after applying for the EIN shown in **A** above, changed its ☐ r
E Election is to be effective for tax year beginning (month, day, year) (see instructions) . . . . .▶
    Caution. A corporation (entity) making the election for its first tax year in existence will usually enter the beginning date of a short tax year that begins on a date other than January 1.
F Selected tax year:

Figure 3-2

If you're keeping score, this is just one small step beyond what it takes to set up a C-corp, and that Form 2553 has no filing fee and can simply be faxed in to the IRS. Take your articles of incorporation and tax ID number to the bank, and you're all set with your corporate bank account—ready to take in your business income and from which you'll be spending all your work-related expenses. There isn't a good or a bad time to do this; it's really based on the business activity you have and whether it justifies the extra efforts and expenses of an S-corp. That said, it's always "cleanest" or ideal to start these off at the beginning of the year, providing you (and your accountant and the IRS) a clean break between you operating as a self-employed individual and you the business. You can, however, start an S-corp at any point in the calendar year and have it apply for that taxable year. What you can't do is get to the end of a year and decide that you want to be an S-corp for the year that just closed. That's why it's important to be heads-up about how you're doing and what your plans are.

What additional costs or responsibilities are involved here? Let's look at each of these in detail:

- You will have an annual report filing with your secretary of state (or whatever agency you filed your incorporation paperwork with). This annual form generally requires a small fee, maybe around $100, and asks you to verify the most basic information about your business. It typically is due on the anniversary of your incorporation. If you need someone else to fill this out for you, you could expect it to take about 30 minutes of their time.

- You will have to file quarterly payroll tax returns to the IRS, your state department of revenue, and your state unemployment agency. *This obligation exists even in quarters for which there is no payroll.* This seems like a bit of a nuisance, but they require forms on file for any quarter you are in operation, even if the forms are full of zeroes. I *strongly* recommend you enlist some help in keeping up with these filings. They happen too often throughout the year, the responsibilities are too great, the changes in laws affecting payroll happen too frequently, and the liabilities for messing it up are too costly. Help in filing your payroll taxes comes in one of a couple forms:
  - **Semi-Service:** This kind of help involves services that will prepare the forms for you, but leave it to you to remember to print them out on time, sign them, mail them, and cut the checks to everyone as needed. This will save you some money versus full service, but it's a bit more responsibility on your end. This might cost you $100-200 a year.
  - **Full Service:** This is the way that most outsourced payroll providers (ADP, for example) would operate. QuickBooks accounting software also has an integrated full-service payroll function. With full service, you can expect them to prepare your forms for you, take full responsibility for filing them on time, and take full responsibility for paying everyone on time and answering questions you have. You can expect this to cost you at least $600-$1,400 a year, depending on the frequency of your payrolls.
- You will have an additional corporate tax return to file at the end of the year. As a self-employed artist, you

were allowed to report your income and expenses on a schedule on your normal individual tax return. Part of the work involved in using an S-corporation is that you split up your activity and report the business income and expenses on a separate tax return and then only show the taxable profit on your personal return. Fees for preparing the corporate return will vary by location and complexity, but you can expect it to cost you at least $400 a year.

So why would anyone want to pay $100 in annual report fees, $600 in payroll tax filings, and $400 for an extra tax return? What does this extra spending buy you? Let's look at an example client and see why setting up the S-corp made sense for him.

CASE STUDY

Mark was a graphic designer and marketing consultant all around town. He had been bringing in an average of $40,000 in income and was able to keep his expenses to about $15,000. His most recent year of operations broke down something like this:

Income	$40,000.00
Expenses:	
Rent	$6,000.00
Telephone	$1,500.00
Computer & Software	$4,500.00
Research	$3,000.00
Total	$15,000.00
Profit (Income-Expenses)	$25,000.00

Figure 3-3

Mark was by no means raking it in just yet, but was able to sustain his lifestyle on that profit of $25,000. As for his tax burden, he was paying 8 percent federal income tax, 3 percent state income tax, and then had self-employment tax to pay at the end of the year on his business profit of 15 percent. This 26 percent of his profit resulted in a combined tax bill for the year of $6,500. Luckily, Mark had set aside 10 percent of all of that income during the year, so he had $4,000 ready to go and only had to hunt down the other $2,500 by April 15. Crisis averted, but then Mark learned that he would have to set aside even more of his income if he was going to avoid getting caught off guard come tax time.

The next year Mark got a surprising call. A marketing firm in LA wanted him to fly out there and take a contract as a consultant, and they were offering him $100,000 to start. But he would be paid as a contractor, not an employee, so the responsibility for taxes fell squarely on his shoulders. Mark gave me a call to discuss his options. We roughed out his expected income and expenses for the coming year:

Income	$100,000.00
Expenses:	
Rent	$12,000.00
Telephone	$1,500.00
Computer & Software	$6,500.00
Research	$4,000.00
Total	$24,000.00
Profit (Income-Expenses)	$76,000.00

Figure 3-4

Even after investing in some upgraded equipment, Mark can only spend $24,000 of his income, leaving him a hefty $76,000 in untaxed income to deal with. At this point, his federal tax rate is projected at 18 percent, his state taxes are 3 percent, and the self-employment tax stays at 15 percent. Whereas he was paying 26 percent last year, he now needs to plan for 36 percent this year. Which amounts to $27,360. Though he has the money to pay the tax, does anyone want to give up 36 percent to the government? Not if you can help it, right? Well, I advised Mark to set up an S-corp in the state of California, and took that same $76,000 he had in profits and divided it up and paid him 50 percent in wages and the other 50 percent as dividends. On the wages, he had to pay payroll taxes (the incorporated equivalent of self-employment taxes), but on the dividends, he didn't have to pay any additional payroll taxes. Just his normal tax rates. So rather than paying payroll taxes on *all* of his $76,000, he only had to pay on $38,000, saving him $38,000 x 15 percent = $5,700. He gladly agreed to the additional $1,100 in annual report and tax filing fees to put $5,700 back in his pocket.

PARTNERSHIP

A partnership can be established in a number of ways, but let's look at the two methods most frequently utilized by artists and creatives. I'll call one the structured approach and the other the unstructured approach. Neither is inherently wrong, but depending on your objectives, you may opt to form using either of these two methods. I'll begin with the unstructured approach so you have a baseline to compare to.

Setting up a partnership can be as simple as two (or three or seven) people getting together and saying, "We're going to go into business together." They may follow with, "You do this, and I'll do that, and it will be amazing." As long as everybody involved agrees to the terms discussed, you have what in the business world is known as a "general partnership." In order to officially establish this general partnership, you only have one filing requirement: request a tax ID number (EIN) from the IRS. With this new tax ID number, you can open a bank account for your partnership, begin selling your products or offering your services, and record all of your expenses. And everyone is equally *entitled to* and *responsible for* the activity of the partnership. What does this mean? If Partner 3 goes out and books a $4,000 job for the group, everyone is entitled to an equal share of that money (after accounting for expenses). Partners 4, 5, and 6 may have had little to do with bringing in the business, yet they all share in the reward. Let's imagine now that Partner 2 decides to go out and buy a touring van, and (in this imaginary world where the auto dealer wouldn't care that the partnership hadn't existed for very long, and granted credit in the business name) the van is financed over six years. He drives it off the lot, and it loses 30 percent of its value instantly. A week later, the band decides they don't like each other anymore and want to break up. Is Partner 2 responsible for the loan he got them into? Yes. And no. The auto dealer can go after *any* member of the general partnership to try to get its money back, including suing any or all of the partners.

What is the much more structured way of handling a partnership? Using an LLC to create the partnership you are looking for. In an LLC (as in an S-corp), the profits of the business are passed through to the owners and they pay the taxes for the business on their personal returns. The difference is that while in an S-corporation the profits are distributed by the ownership percentage of each shareholder (the number of shares of stock they hold), in an LLC, you can divide the profits and tax liability by almost anything you like. Take the example of a small indie film project that is going to be conceived, shot, and produced by one woman. She has a friend who wants to finance the whole thing. In an S-corp, if the filmmaker doesn't contribute equal capital to the company, she's not entitled to an equal share of the company. The friend would own the whole thing. But in an LLC, the *work* of the filmmaker is allowed to balance out the *money* of the other party, and they can be viewed as equals.

Creating an LLC for use by a partnership involves two steps: applying for the tax ID and filing articles of formation in the state in which you will operate—only one additional step to setting up a general partnership. In many states, you needn't even list out all the owners. For those states, you won't have to sort all that out until you file your first partnership tax return. But now comes another key component of any functioning LLC: the partnership operating agreement. This is not legally required, but you *should* think of it as a requirement. And you will ask your attorney to help you create it (see the section called "Your Team" to follow). Why is this document so important? Because we all know that the number of bands that have stayed together until death did them part is far less than the number that parted ways somewhere down the road. The same goes for most businesses of any kind. And the partnership agreement will address that circumstance and a number of other issues. A good agreement will at least discuss:

- **Name:** Seems self-explanatory, but it's good to all agree in writing, correct?
- **Purpose:** Do you want to prevent your business from getting off course? Like your bridal boutique from getting into taxidermy as well?
- **Ownership Percentages:** What are they to begin with, and how are they valued, added, and sold over time?
- **Exits:** Under what conditions can someone leave the partnership? Or when can they be *forced* out? What happens?

- **Voting:** Who's in charge? What kinds of things can be decided on the fly? What needs unanimous consent of everyone?
- **Distributions:** How is the money going to be split up? When and how much?
- **Taxes:** Who picks up the tax bill and in what percentages? Will the company distribute to the partners to help them pay for it?
- **Winding Down:** What happens when everyone wants out? Or if five out of eight want out?
- **Indemnification:** Want everyone to be responsible for their own actions instead of equally liable as in the example of the car loan above?

These are not things anyone wakes up excited to talk about. Or even think about. Usually, getting a business off the ground—whether it's an art gallery or a design house or a new band—is the most exciting time for everyone involved. You had a great idea, and it's time to make it real. So this conversation is in many ways the equivalent of signing that prenuptial agreement right after deciding to get married. Nobody wants to assume the worst, but you could be prepared for it. It's guaranteed to be an easier conversation at the beginning of the business than it will be when some people aren't on speaking terms and there's real money and history involved.

Want to see how this played out in real life for some clients of ours?

CASE STUDY

Sarah came into my office one year to get her personal taxes done. She had a part-time day job that paid her as an employee, took out taxes, and issued her a W2 along the way. Then she had a list of what she called self-employed income and expenses. I asked her what she did, and she explained that she and a few friends had started a website where they sold custom furniture online. There were four designers in total, but they didn't do a whole lot of planning up front and just kind of started selling things. When the bank or PayPal or anyone wanted to know info about the business, Sarah used her name and her social security number and her address. So all of this income and all of the expenses were left for her to report. Her partners would have no responsibilities taxwise at all. That hardly seemed fair.

I advised Sarah that for the coming year, she set up an LLC and make each designer a 25 percent partner. They would first get paid out directly for the work they did, and then any money that was left after expenses would be split equally. Most importantly, the tax burden would be equally shared by all four partners. This appropriately shifted thousands of dollars of taxes off Sarah's return and split it equally among the partners. I also helped her and her attorney draft a partnership agreement that allowed for any possible situation we could imagine. The partnership now had its own legal structure, its own bank account, and its own tax ID number. We had effectively severed this entity from one of its owners.

What about films? LLCs are very often used in the world of film and movie production. In fact, a production company that releases several projects will often have each individual film set up as its own LLC. And all those baby LLCs are owned by a parent LLC. Why create all this mess? Let's look at another example.

- -

CASE STUDY

I had a film-production operation come to me with what they thought were some simple needs. They had three projects about to be funded, and their sound guy (of all people) told them all they needed to do was set up an LLC and get started. Luckily, they sought out confirmation of the sound guy's advice and asked me for an opinion. (Disclaimer: No offense to sound guys. I am a former sound guy.) I started out the conversation by mapping out what they wanted to do. They told me about the three projects that were funded and ready to begin production. Then I asked them some questions about how they were going to do things and decided that they needed not one, but *four* LLCs. I'll let you eavesdrop on our conversation.

"So for these three films, are there the same number of investors in each?"

"No. One has two investors and the other two have three investors each."

"And do they have the same ownership stake in each project?"

"No, they actually vary with every project and the funding we needed and the order in which we approached people."

"So if you only had one entity to work with, how would you make each of them have the right percentage ownership?"

"I see."

"And if one film becomes profitable, are you going to make the investors wait until the company overall is profitable to pay them out?"

"No, they're going to expect a return once the one project makes money. They are thinking of each of these as separate investments—not an investment in our production company."

I drew up a model for them that looked like this:

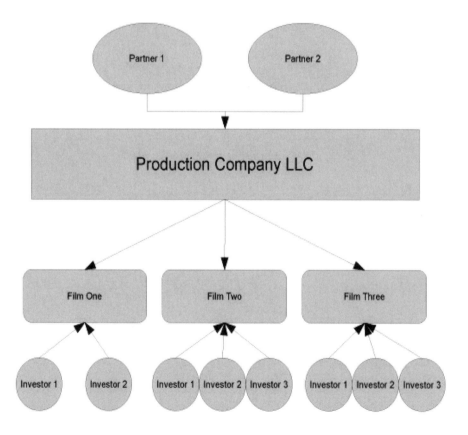

Figure 3-5

The two partners in the production company would each own 50 percent of the parent LLC. And the parent LLC got to keep ownership of 30 percent of each of the three projects it was doing. The remaining 70 percent ownership of each movie was split up among the investors. It was the best way for the production company to keep clean books on each project independently. It amounted to an additional $750 in renewal fees each year, but for them that expense was well worth the peace of mind that they had accounted for everything correctly. There's no faster way to have investors stop returning your calls than to lose track of their money. And there's no better way to get them to come back again and again than to show them you are a trustworthy steward of their investment.

LLCS: MAJOR MYTHS DEBUNKED

Okay. I'm not trying to pick on LLCs without cause. When used effectively, an LLC can make a lot of sense for some activities. But what are the biggest informational challenges to overcome when looking at an LLC as a vehicle for your business? Well, for starters:

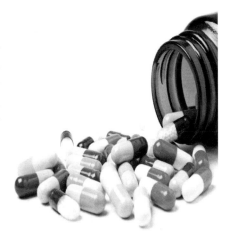

Figure 3-6

- LLCs are commonly recommended by attorneys in the same way that antibiotics are commonly recommended by doctors. It's broad-spectrum and an easy answer that *technically speaking* isn't *wrong* in very many situations. But often a little patience and discovery of what your real business model is like will result in a decision that is less expensive and does everything for you that an LLC could do.
- LLC stands for "limited liability corporation," and there is a large misconception that it is the only form of business that limits your liability. In fact, *any* form of

business that includes the word *corporation* is going to have the same liability protection that an LLC affords you. That includes C-corporations, S-corporations, and LLCs (and even limited liability partnerships if you want to get technical about it). Once you have put the "corporate wall" around your business activity, it doesn't matter what kind of corporation it is. The fact remains that *it* is no longer *you*. And that is what limited liability is all about.

• Google runs the world. I will assert this premise. And when you search phrases such as "start my own business" or "set up business" or the like, you are bound to be overrun with ads and links trying to get you to set up an LLC. Why? Why do most things that you see right away in Google show up first? Because they generate the most money for people. Incorporation sites, just like attorneys, are likely to suggest structures that have the highest fees in order to make *their* fees look lower. And again, because technically they're not wrong. There's just often a better answer.

And what is that better answer? Well, let me start instead with the instances where setting up an LLC *does* make sense. *LLCs are a good tool to create what is meant to be a true partnership—where several people or businesses gather together, and work to build something they wish to share in equally.* I'll give you a couple of examples in practice:

A band is often formed as a partnership, and I'm not opposed to this structure for bands for a few reasons. First, the members of a band often wear a lot of hats—one is the sound guy/lighting designer, one is the lead singer/songwriter/marketing director, one is the drummer/booking agent, another is the keyboard player/merchandise creator. There is very little time available for filling out forms or dealing with an accountant on a quarterly basis. And an LLC allows the band to carry on their year with very little thought put into the tax side of their business. They pay out to each other what each band member deserves; they all share in the profit or loss at the end of the year. And if one or another member needs to leave, there can be easy rules put in place to govern just such a situation. This is where the partnership agreement you've drafted will be an excellent reference to you.

The other situation in which I've set up partnerships for people in the past is the "collective"-type operation. Think of a handmade-goods collective: several creatives all doing their thing, coming together to rent out a storefront, with collective marketing efforts, all in the goal of selling as much of everyone's goods as possible. Or a "design shop" with graphic designers, front-end designers, web developers, back-end coders, typographers, and so forth. In either case, you can have multiple people owning various percentages of the company, each getting paid out only for the work that they do, and all sharing in the bottom line according to whatever allotment you see fit.

But LLCs seldom make sense for the one-person business. A one-person LLC by default is treated as a "disregarded entity," meaning it exists for legal purposes but doesn't exist for tax purposes. You would continue to file the income and expenses of your activity on Schedule C of your individual tax return. This is okay in some cases, particularly for small and early-stage operations where the owner is just really concerned with protecting his or her liability. However, usually when a one-person entity such as a photographer or actress or model is looking to set up a business around him- or herself, it's because he or she is looking to get some tax benefits out of it. And that can't be accomplished with an LLC alone. In those cases, an S-corporation is often the least expensive and most direct way to maximize your benefit.

LET'S REALLY COMPARE THEM

	Sole Prop	S-Corp	C-Corp	Partnership
Tracking Income / Expenses	Spreadsheet / Outright.com	QuickBooks	QuickBooks	QuickBooks / Freshbooks
Where reported?	1040, Schedule C	1120S—> 1040s	1120	1065—>1040s
Who pays?	Owner	Owners	Business	Owners
How paid?	Income / SE Tax	Income / Payroll Taxes	Income / Payroll / Dividends	Income / SE Tax
Income range	Neg - $30k	$30k - $275k	$275k +	any

Figure 3-7

Let's discuss these differences briefly so you can use this chart to your advantage. First let's look at a sole proprietorship. As you recall, this is the most common form of business for artists and creative professionals and anyone who calls themselves "self-employed," "freelance," or "independent contractors." As far as tracking income and expenses, there are a number of options out there, but you're not going to need a system that is overly excessive. I recommend sticking to a simple spreadsheet that tracks your income and expenses *by category*. That sorting by category will be critical to your year-end tax prep process, since that's how you have to total up and report your activity for tax purposes. If you want to look at a slight upgrade from the spreadsheet, take a look at Outright.com. This service is designed particularly for self-employed people and has features that no other personal finance tool will include (such as keeping track of your self-employment taxes). At year end, all this activity will land on Schedule C of your personal tax return, where you—the owner—will report the income and expenses. You will be responsible for income taxes as well as self-employment taxes on that business profit—all of which will be a part of your year-end tax bill. This form of business serves those operating at a loss particularly well because there is nothing between your loss and yourself. You get to claim it all directly against your other income. And it's appropriate up to about $30K in business profit (income less expenses). At that point, an S-corp can start to pose significant tax benefits worth exploring.

The S-corp will require that you step up to some more robust (or grown-up, if you want to think of it that way) tax software. With the S-corp, you will have such things accruing as owner distribution payments, and a number of other transactions that are really neither income nor expense. That's where the spreadsheet or Outright will leave you hanging. Most simple tracking systems look at two things: money in and money out. They struggle with accounting for the complexities of a corporation, and you will have to get some real accounting software. At year end, you'll report the income and expenses on Form 1120S, which will show all business income and all the related expenses and arrive at a bottom-line figure. That amount is then split up among the owners by ownership percentage, and each will report his or her share of the profit or loss on his or her individual tax return. While the business itself pays no income tax, the owners will pay the government in two ways: personal income tax and also in the form of payroll taxes (the same social security and Medicare taxes that comprise self-employment tax plus unemployment taxes). However, with the ability to control the throttle on how much profit is considered wages, you stand to benefit from some savings on these taxes once you've reached about $30K in profit. And this is a workable system all the way up to about $275,000 or so in profit annually. At that point, you will start to feel the burden of paying for the tax liability of the business on your personal return, especially if you can't distribute *all* of that profit to yourself. In other words, you could wind up being responsible for paying taxes on business profit that you haven't passed along to yourself yet because you need it to stay in the business. Now it might become preferable for the business to pay taxes for itself, as in a C-corporation.

To do you justice, a C-corp will require a real accounting package such as QuickBooks for all the same reasons as an S-corp. However, the main difference will be in how the information is reported and paid for. The C-corp will report all business income and expenses, but will also calculate and pay for its own income taxes. The business owners are responsible only for paying income taxes on dividends and income, and payroll taxes on wages paid. This is that double-level taxation scheme that many find unfavorable, but again, if you are raking in $1 million in profits, the tax burdens alone will be too much for any one individual to bear in a given year. Accordingly, most large corporations (such as those traded on the stock exchanges) are set up as C-corporations. The business pays its own taxes out of its profits, employees pay taxes on their wages, and the owners or investors pay taxes on the dividends or interest they receive from the business.

A partnership can be an interesting animal. Some are very small, some are very large. Accordingly, a number of types of systems for tracking income and expenses might be appropriate. At a basic level, there are a variety of options available to you. A simple spreadsheet might actually do the trick, provided you are dedicated and responsible enough to keep up with it. If you want a little more support, you could turn to a simple and online-based system such as Freshbooks to track your activity. QuickBooks is also a viable option—and might be recommended to more complex partnerships—but could be overkill for a business with simple income and expenses. Remember, anytime you are spending on this side of your business is time you're not spending doing what you're best at. So it's important to be as realistic about your needs as possible. The activity you tally up will be reported on Form 1065, which, like the S-corp return, will show the income and expenses and indicate how the profit or loss is to be shared among the members of the LLC.

The difference again is that in the LLC, you have control to dictate how the split is calculated: based on capital contributed or work done or anything you like. Ultimately the owners will pick up the tax bill for the business profit on their individual returns and will pay both income and self-employment taxes on that money, much like a multimember sole proprietorship. This is great for smaller partnerships, where the self-employment tax burden is not great, because you get the benefit of pass-through taxation without the responsibility of filing quarterly payroll tax returns. And although that self-employment tax can become a force to be reckoned with, partnerships are a viable structure for almost any size business.

ADVANTAGES TO FORMING A SEPARATE BUSINESS

Figure 3-8

So what are the primary advantages to setting up a business that exists outside of yourself? It will take a little more homework on your end, and will result in an awful lot more mail coming to you from the government—but if you can keep a clear head about all of that, then here are a few of the benefits you will reap:

A separate business structure will remove all of the activity from your social security number. No longer will you have to hand out your social security number to anyone who wants you to fill out a W9 for your $800 check. Your personal income is your personal income, and your business income—well, that's now under its own roof. And that kind of clarity can feel really good when your life gets as hectic as it does.

A separate business can have its own name. Have you come up with a really clever name for your copywriting agency? For your band? For your new film? Are you tired of getting people really excited about that branding and marketing you did to create that image and then having to say, "Uh . . . could you make that out to Cheryll Jenkins???" By setting up a legal entity that's living and breathing outside of yourself, you are able to give it any name you want. And in the process, you are able to sign contracts, make websites, hand out business cards, and in general, carry on in whatever name you like.

A separate business can have its own bank account. Similar to your business having its own name, its having a separate bank account and credit cards is key to keeping your records straight. This simple change will let you ignore what happens in your personal account—that's now your own personal business. Instead, all of your business activity will be concentrated in one place, nice and easy. Eventually, you'll be able to build up your own business credit and apply for loans and such directly as a business as well. Take out a car loan, buy a building . . .

A separate business can involve significant tax savings. Depending on your circumstances, as I've discussed in the last few chapters, you may be able to save thousands in self-employment taxes by setting yourself up as an S-corporation, C-corporation, or LLC. The choice is ultimately best reviewed with an attorney and accountant who can assess your personal circumstances. Unfortunately, it would be imprudent to make broad recommendations in this book, because each of you is like a snowflake. Everyone has a number of particulars about his or her life that can make or break the decision about which form of business is the right one. The best thing you can do is get as educated as you can about it (Hey! Good start!) and then sit down with *both an attorney and an accountant* to get a recommendation. It will be well worth your time and money. Mistakes made in how you set up are often far costlier than getting the advice you need at the beginning.

THE BUSINESS CALENDAR OF IMPORTANT DATES

For a C- or S-corporation or partnership, there is a slightly more involved calendar of important dates to add to your calendar for the year. Involving things such as payroll will add to your filing responsibilities, but just remember—you're going to pay other people to worry about those payroll deadlines for you! I'm just including it so you can hold them to task if they slip up. All dates are consistent year to year, except when they fall on weekends or holidays. In those cases, just push the deadline forward to the next business day. And I've noted on each date whether it applies to [C]-corporations, [S]-corporations, and/or [P]artnerships.

- **JANUARY**
  - **15 (S/P): Individual Estimated Tax Payment #4:** This is the final installment of your prior year's estimated tax payments. (Remember, these payments apply to cases where you accumulate over $1,000 in tax liability over the course of the year.)
  - **31 (C/S/P): 1099 and W2 Deadline #1:** This is the deadline to provide W2s to your employees and 1099s to your independent contractors. There is a separate deadline (to follow) for furnishing these forms to the IRS, which will allow you to correct any mistakes employees bring up.
  - **31 (C/S): Q4 Payroll Tax Filings Due:** Payroll tax forms for the fourth quarter of the previous year are due. These include IRS Forms 940 and 941, along with

state unemployment and state income tax withholding forms.

- **FEBRUARY**
  - **28 (C/S/P): 1099 and W2 Deadline #2:** One month after needing to send W2s and 1099s to your employees and contractors, you will now have to send in the final copies to the IRS and Social Security Administration. Don't forget W3s and 1096s—these are the "cover sheets" that accompany W2s and 1099s and let the government know how many forms to expect.

- **MARCH**
  - **15 (C/S): Corporate Tax Return:** This is the original deadline to file your C-Corporation Form 1120 or S-Corporation Form 1120S. Alternatively, you can file Form 7004 to obtain an automatic six-month extension.
  - **15 (S): S-Corp Election:** If you want to be treated as an S-corporation for the current year, this is the last date you can make that election take effect. Otherwise you'll be waiting until next year.

- **APRIL**
  - **15 (C): Corporate Estimated Payment #1:** This is the first installment of your current-year C-corporation estimated payments.
  - **15 (C/S/P): Individual Income Tax Return:** This is the due date for your individual return (Form 1040) or the extension (Form 4868). Remember that extending your return buys you an extra six months to file but not to pay, so if you have a balance due, you may want to get an estimate of your payment on file at this point even if you don't complete the return. Not doing so creates interest from this date until you pay.
  - **15 (S/P): Individual Estimated Tax Payment #1:** This is your first payment toward your current-year tax liability.
  - **15 (P): Partnership Tax Return:** April 15 is the deadline for your Form 1065 Partnership tax return, which will show your income and expenses and distrib-

utable amounts to all partners. Or file Form 7004 to
obtain an automatic five-month extension.

- ○ **30 (C/S): Q1 Payroll Tax Filings Due:** Payroll tax
  forms for the first quarter of this year are due. These
  include IRS Form 941, state unemployment, and state
  income tax withholding forms.
- **MAY** (none)
- **JUNE**
  - ○ **15 (C): Corporate Estimated Payment #2:** This is
    the second installment of your current-year C-corpora-
    tion estimated payments.
  - ○ **15 (S/P): Individual Estimated Tax Payment
    #2:** This is your second payment toward your current-
    year tax liability.
- **JULY**
  - ○ **31 (C/S): Q2 Payroll Tax Filings Due:** Payroll tax
    forms for the second quarter of this year are due. These
    include IRS Form 941, state unemployment, and state
    income tax withholding forms.
- **AUGUST** (none)
- **SEPTEMBER**
  - ○ **15 (S/P): Individual Estimated Tax Payment
    #3:** This is your third payment toward your current-
    year tax liability.
  - ○ **15 (P): Partnership Tax Return Extension Dead-
    line:** If you filed for an extension on your partnership
    return, the final return is due today, including sending
    out K-1s to all partners.
  - ○ **15 (C/S): Corporate Tax Return Extension
    Deadline:** Extended S-corporation and C-corporation
    returns are due on this day. S-corporations must also
    furnish K-1s to shareholders today.
  - ○ **15 (C): Corporate Estimated Payment #3:** This is
    the third installment of your current-year C-corporation
    estimated payments.
- **OCTOBER**
  - ○ **15 (C/S/P): Individual Income Tax Return Ex-**

tension Deadline: If you filed an extension in April of this year, your individual tax return is due six months later on October 15.

○ **31 (C/S): Q3 Payroll Tax Filings Due:** Payroll tax forms for the third quarter of this year are due. These include IRS Form 941, state unemployment, and state income tax withholding forms.

• **NOVEMBER** (none)
• **DECEMBER**

○ **15 (C): Corporate Estimated Payment #4:** This is the fourth installment of your current-year C-corporation estimated payments.

Remember, if you'd like the links to automatically add these dates to your calendar, you can find them here: http://www.rockstarcpa.com/minding-your-business.

LET'S MAP IT OUT (INCOME, EXPENSES, TAXES)

Okay. Now let's attempt to look at the big picture for both partnerships and S-corporations. This roadmap should help you visualize the overall flow of income and expenses to the business and ultimately to each of you—the partners or shareholders.

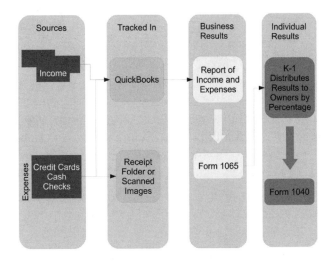

Figure 3-9

I'll begin with a partnership. Income and expenses will be tracked in your accounting system (QuickBooks for the sake of this example). That is where the majority of data collection and effort will take place. The remaining paper trail can be stashed in a folder or scanned and saved electronically. At year end, the accounting system will dump out a report for you detailing your income and expenses by category. This report is what fuels the partnership tax-return preparation. All those income and expenses are reported on Form 1065, and the resulting profit or loss is split up among the partners and reported to them on Form K-1. Each owner takes that form and incorporates it into his or her individual tax return, and the case is closed.

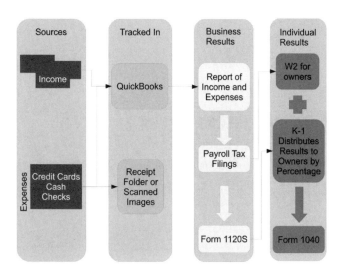

Figure 3-10

In an S-corporation, income and expenses are similarly tracked in QuickBooks or some other accounting package. Any paper receipts or invoices get stored in a file or electronically. The accounting system will output a report of all your income and expenses, which will drive two things: your payroll tax filings and your corporate tax return. The payroll filings result in the owners getting a W2, just as you would from any other job. And the corporate tax return results in a net profit that gets split up among all owners and passed on to them on a Form K-1. The owner(s) then take the resulting W2 and K-1 and add them to their individual tax returns to complete the picture.

Study Questions

1. Which of the three forms of business discussed in this section involves double taxation?
2. Under what circumstances is a C-corporation preferable to a partnership or S-corporation?
3. How can an S-corporation reduce your overall tax bill versus being self-employed? At what level of profit does that take place?
4. Who is responsible for the actions of a general partnership?
5. What document helps partners in an LLC define how they are going to work together?
6. What are the four main advantages to setting up a business entity outside of yourself?

Answers

1. A C-corporation has taxation both at the corporate and the individual level. The business pays for its profit, and then when the owners distribute what's left as wages or dividends, they are taxed personally.
2. A C-corporation can be preferable in a business where the profit created in a year generates a tax bill too high for the owners to bear personally. Typically, this means $275,000 or more in profit a year.
3. An S-corporation reduces your tax bill by replacing self-employment taxes with payroll taxes—often at 50 percent of the cost to you. This reduction tends to offset any additional costs of being incorporated at around $30,000 a year in profit.
4. All partners are jointly and severally liable for the actions of any partner.
5. A partnership agreement. This document is so critical to your operations that getting an attorney involved is highly recommended.
6. A unique tax ID number that masks your social security number, the ability to use whatever name you want and

get paid in that name, the ability to open a bank account in the name of the business, and the potential for some tax savings.

4

Tracking Expenses: The Artist's Third-Most Important Job

WHO CARES?

Wow. After all that talk about the Five-Year Rule and self-employment versus incorporation, let's bring it all back and get real for a minute. Let's ask a very important question: who cares?

Figure 4-1

Seriously, who cares about all this? Can't I just do what I love and forget about all the money of it and just deal with the government if and when they come knocking on my door? After all, people fly under the radar all the time. Artists are broke anyway. What would anyone care what I do?

Well, the short answer is that people care that are important enough to be dangerous to your career. The longer answer requires more explanation. Your agent/manager/business manager may care about your income and expenses because that is how *they* determine their income. In the same way that you expect the door guy to do an accurate job collecting money from people so you get paid your share, those who help support your career also rely on you for their careers. Those people should be your closest allies, and accordingly you should take care of them. Enough said.

The next group that cares is the government. Why am I talking about expenses and not income here? Because the government makes sure they get as much information as possible to collect at least the *mini-*

mum amount you earned. And frankly, they don't care if you overreport your income. More taxes for them. (Though if you wait long enough they will eventually send that check back.) It is entirely your responsibility to report your expenses as accurately as possible and be able to support them with backup. (I'll talk more about the appropriate backup momentarily.) The IRS can be dangerous because if they get suspicious of your claims and starting asking you for backup, that process can be long and burdensome. Later in this book you'll learn about how to turn the IRS into your friends—and why that's the best strategy.

The third group of people interested in your expenses is what I'll refer to as "the business." For a musician, this is your record label. For writers, this is your publisher. For bloggers, this is your advertising syndicate. "The business" cares about what you make because they are interested in the viability of your career. At some point, you will want to be able to demonstrate to these entities that you have what it takes to make it. Financial stability can go a long way toward making that point. As you remember from "The Five-Year Rule," being able to prove that you take the financial aspect of your art seriously is always appreciated by the IRS as well. In general, your labels and publishers and tour managers will be happier with someone who is making decent money and doing a bang-up job of treating his or her career professionally than someone who is raking it in and blowing off all of his or her responsibilities. That just makes life harder on everyone around them.

And *even if* you don't have an agent or business manager or publisher or label, everyone has this last person in their lives: you—the artist. If you don't start caring about keeping track of your deductions, you will have a difficult time creating a long-term successful career for yourself. For many reasons. Most importantly:

a) You need to start caring about where your money is going. I don't care how much or how little it is. If you aren't making much, it should be that much more important to you to find out where each of those pennies and dollars end up. Because while yes, it's all about the art in the end, if you aren't able to sustain yourself in the long run, you'll be back in the world of "straight jobs" much earlier than you'd like to be. So help keep the circus in town, and get serious about your money.

It's like in *Zen and the Art of Motorcycle Maintenance* when Robert Pirsig is describing the difference between *riding* a motorcycle and *maintaining* a motorcycle. Riding is the romantic part of it, the actual action, the doing, the fun. That's your art: your books, your dance, your concerts, your film. Maintenance is the classic part of it, the form behind the romance, the nuts and bolts, the "boring" stuff—but that's just it. When you start looking at not one or the other, but instead thinking of the interrelationship and how each supports the other, the nuts and bolts aren't really "boring" at all. Enough of that though. I'm no real philosopher. Even for those who are comfortable enough to pay other people to worry about their money and expenses for them—you need to start caring as well. For whatever reason (and this is completely anecdotal), I have experienced that my most successful clients in terms of career or artistic recognition also have their finances together the most. Coincidence? Maybe. But I definitely don't think so. Worst case, that "adviser" you paid to take care of things for you makes mistakes year after year that go unnoticed because you don't care, and you wind up in jail for tax evasion (just think Wesley Snipes).

b) This is part of the deal. You don't get to be President of the United States without going completely gray after three years and agreeing to sleep no more than four hours a night. You don't get to be on television in the Olympics without sacrificing friends and fun day in, day out, for your craft. And you don't get to tell people you're a professional musician, or say "I'm in a band," or that you're a film producer, or that you're a professional actor, or get to quit your day job to write novels full time, without putting in your share of work on the business. As Fredrick Douglas said, "There is no progress without struggle." You too won't enjoy progress in your artistic career without taking the money seriously. You are one of 3 percent of Americans who go to work every day saying, "I love what I do for a living." No, you don't have to feel guilty about that, but you should also not complain about tracking your Broadway theater tickets as business expenses.

So why is this your third-most important job? Well, your art is always No. 1. Not even I, your money-minded accountant, will argue that. And I have to imagine there is something else that is more important than this—even if I can't think of it right now. But third? Definitely third-most important.

WELL THEN, HOW DO I DO IT?

Good question. This is a two-part world you have to navigate. There's the physical-world side, for which I would recommend as simple a solution as you can stand. Here's why: because you aren't going to want to spend a random Sunday afternoon mulling over receipts for the sake of memory. And as your accountant, I don't really need to see them either. In general, the only people interested in the backup of your expenses is the IRS. And since the likelihood they will call upon you is slim, we don't want to waste more time studying for the test than we need to. Most people will be able to get away with a twelve-month accordion folder you can buy at any office store. Save your receipts as you go, and then after they've been entered, just drop them in that month. Month's over, move on the next one. Done. For the computer-world side of things, there are many options out there, and really you should find a solution that works best for you in terms of the following aspects:

- **Features:** Will range from the simplest systems to the most complex. Generally speaking, as your career progresses, so does the complexity of your "business," and so too will the complexity of your tracking system.
- **Ease of Use:** Maybe you are the computer gamer/ Nintendo nerd graphic-designer type. Or maybe you're the never-seen-an-iPhone/still-have-a-calendar-in-a-spiral-notebook graphic-designer type. I've met them both and worked with both. And many in between. I wouldn't recommend the same systems to them, because if the system isn't comfortable enough for you to use, you won't use it anyway.
- **Cost:** Tracking your income and expenses is necessary for the reasons above, but it should also never really get

in the way of your art financially. So make sure to keep your accounting system in line with the rest of your budget.

- **Ability to Connect:** Similar to "Ease of Use," the system that will work best of you is also one that is most seamlessly integrated into your daily life. For example, if you already have well-established relationships with one or another bank, it would be great for your system to be able to "talk" to your bank and automatically pull your transactions from there, no? Yes. It would. Likewise, if you despise Internet Explorer and give people strange looks when they don't know what a Firefox is, it would probably make sense to use a system that is compatible with the browser you sit in front of 80 percent of the day.

So it's clearly a very personal decision/recommendation. But I will attempt to break down a few basic forms, and you can modify from there. Or seek the help of a professional to make a more personalized recommendation. I will call my three general categories Apprentice, Artist, and Master.

- **Apprentice:** For artists who are just beginning their careers, you may not have a large enough volume of transactions to demand a system that is high on the "Features" scale. It may also be important to keep your system low on the "Cost" scale. But it is important for you to take it seriously, and to get in a routine of updating your records. For you, a system based on a simple spreadsheet will do the trick. And the cost of $0 should be right up your alley. Just head over to http://www.rockstarcpa.com/minding-your-business, and you will be able to download a sheet to use that is prefilled with categories for your type of artistry. Can't get easier than that.
- **Artist:** If once a month is not reasonable for you because you are accumulating too many transactions a

month—or if you are the kind of person who wants a little more control over reporting and so forth—then I would recommend stepping up to a web-based program that will help you automate many of the aspects of record keeping. Mint.com, though designed for personal finance, can be rigged up to keep decent track of your business income and expenses. Outright.com is an even more developed system that has many of the eases of use that Mint.com incorporates, but Outright is designed specifically for self-employed folks. You can find discounted links for Outright.com at http://bit.ly/Jy1wxU. Or a basic setup of QuickBooks might do the trick for you. QuickBooks is the most commonly used small-business accounting software out there—and not without reason. It's been around the block the most times, had the most improvement cycles, is relatively intuitive, and is scalable (you can get more advanced versions as you grow that connect seamlessly). And luckily for you, by going to Rockstarcpa.com and signing up for our monthly newsletter, you will receive a welcome e-mail that includes a link to a trial of the most basic version of QuickBooks for the specially discounted price of $0. Man, you have it good.

- **Master:** If you have progressed beyond being self-employed and have set up a separate legal entity (incorporated, LLC, etc.), then it's time to step up to full-blown versions of some accounting software. The biggest reason is that you now have to deal with transactions that go beyond simple income and expenses—such as payroll taxes, shareholder dividends, equity contributions, lines of credit, and so forth. Simpler systems are not designed to handle those kinds of transactions. In the QuickBooks family, you would step up to QuickBooks Pro or QuickBooks for Mac—which, back in 2009, received a major facelift and is now much closer to its PC counterpart than it had been in the past. For you, Master, sadly no more freebies. *But,* I will share a special discount link with you when you sign up for my newsletter at Rockstarcpa.com.

AND WHAT SHOULD I KEEP TRACK OF?

Earlier in the book, I discussed what I would do and what I wouldn't. And though I promised not to provide a huge laundry list of deductions, I do want to go through a few basic things you should understand (especially those that I feel there are misconceptions about). But I will say this first: *When in doubt, keep it and keep track of it.* Yes, important enough to italicize. Why? It's always better for a client to come to me with too much and let me say something like, "No, unfortunately we probably won't write off your doggie daycare." The worst is hearing a client say, "Well, there was probably another $1,000 in expenses here or there but I just don't know what happened to the receipts." If you wouldn't literally take $250 and throw it out onto the street for no reason, you should also not be "okay" with missing $1,000 in deductions that could have well been yours.

In the coming sections of this chapter, I will review some general small-business deductions, some artist-specific hotspots, some frequently disseminated myths, and the Golden Rule of Deductions. Although entire books have been written on deductions alone, reading this chapter should prove to you why those books are relatively unnecessary.

GENERAL BUSINESS EXPENSES

Yes, the fact that you have to treat yourself like a business means lots of extra work such as tracking your income and expenses, but luckily for you, it also means you get to write off a lot of the same things any business can. So before you launch into another diatribe about the evils of corporate tax breaks, let's talk about a few that you can enjoy first:

- **Computer Equipment:** This includes the cost of purchasing, operating, repairing, and all accessories. It will be up to you or your tax preparer to determine what percentage of the use is business related and also whether to deduct the cost all within the same year or spread it out over a few years.

- **Office Furniture:** You better believe the folks at NBC are writing off the cost of their five-figure chairs in their boardroom. Likewise, you and I will write off our $120 chair from Office Depot. Or if you can afford a nice workstation, it may be a substantial enough expense to break up the cost and deduct over a period of a few years.

- **Software:** If you have to buy any software to do what it is you do—whether for graphic design, video editing, lighting design, script writing, or whatever—it too is a deductible expense. That copy of NBA 2K10 that you use for a little R&R? Probably not. But if you write video game reviews, that might be a different story . . . Software is typically broken up and deducted over a three-year period.

- **Accounting:** Yep, the cost of your twelve-month accordion folder, your QuickBooks program—heck, even this book are all deductible. And throw in the cost of your tax prep as well. And any other tax or accounting help you get throughout the year.

- **Bank Fees:** Does your bank hit you with a monthly service charge that you just don't understand, but also don't have the cosmic energy to fight each time? Well if it's on your business bank account, you can at least write it off.

- **Conferences:** Again, it's not just for rich doctors. You too can find industry-related conferences and write off the cost of the trip, as well as the conference fees. These are sometimes great opportunities to showcase your work, or sometimes just places to learn new techniques and meet new people. But the important thing to learn here is that you can definitely deduct the cost. *(N.B. If you mix a little pleasure into your business, be careful to track the ratio of work to play, as you will multiply all your costs by that ratio to figure out your deduction.)*

- **Education:** Continuing education is required in many professions, but is just a good idea across the board. It's no different for an artist. If you need to take a few voice lessons a year just to stretch out the money-maker, or you regularly attend master classes at this local university, the cost of keeping sharp will be fully deductible on your taxes.

- **Gifts:** It's limited to $25 per person—and they have to be business associates. Can't include your Christmas present for Grandma. But you want to buy your three literary agents a Starbucks gift card to help them get through your novel? Go ahead, and make sure to write it off.

- **Home Office:** The rules about this have loosened a bit, though this is still a highly contested area. The rule is no longer that it has to be a completely separate room with doors. What remains, however, are two important qualities: it has to be *exclusively* and *regularly* used for your business. Take the square footage of that space and divide it by your entire home or apartment square footage, and that is the percentage of your rent, property tax, mortgage interest, renter's or homeowner's insurance, gas, electric, water, and telephone costs.

Figure 4-2

- **Internet Expenses:** I may differ from a few CPAs on this one, but I firmly believe that Internet costs should be deducted 100 percent for business, regardless if part of the use is personal. The reason is this: the cost of the connection typically doesn't increase based on your use. The personal amount of Internet use doesn't increase your expense, and accordingly should not cost you any part of your deduction.

- **Meals and Entertainment:** There are three kinds of meals to keep track of. The first I will call "travel" meals. As discussed below, when you are traveling out of town overnight, your meals are 100 percent deductible. Just throw these deductions into the travel category for that reason. The other two kinds of meals will be 50 percent deductible. The second is what I'll call "networking" meals. These are the dinners or drinks with agents, cast members, directors, interviewees, and the like. The third category, also 50 percent deductible, is what I'll call "working" meals. This includes both when you order a pizza to the studio because you just can't stop working tonight and need to meet this deadline, and the situation where you have an audition at 10 am and swing through the drive-thru on your way to a 1pm rehearsal. Your work schedule prevented you from being able to eat at home, and accordingly, it's a deductible expense. The key is it has to be bookended by work—if you meet that test, you can write it off even if it's just you eating alone.

- **Office Supplies:** Boring, but deductible. So get organized.

- **Parking:** Not for everything, but for work-related needs, yes. And not to park at home, and not at your day job. But parking for auditions, at the theater every night for rehearsal, meters and lots across the country while you're on tour—definitely.

- **Subcontractors:** Side musicians, understudies, apprentice designers, assistants, and so forth. Anytime

you have to take a part of what you were paid and parse
it out to someone else, you are going to write it off. (Keep
in mind that if you pay an individual over $600 in a
calendar year, you will also need to send him or her a
1099 in January of the following year.)

- **Travel:** The IRS defines travel as staying overnight in
  a city different than your "tax home" city. While you are
  traveling, all costs of your meals, transportation, lodging,
  and so forth are deductible. For those with extensive road
  schedules, discuss with your tax preparer whether using
  per diem rates will be more advantageous for you.
- **Vehicle:** You may not have the fleet of trucks that
  Wal-Mart does, but you too can deduct the cost of your
  vehicle. Or at least the business part of it. Auto expenses
  are dealt with in one of two ways: by using a standard
  mileage rate or by using your actual expenses. Since you
  get to use the bigger of the two numbers, it's always best
  to track both all year and compare at the end. If you
  have a smart phone and want a little extra help keeping
  track of the mileage, check out this app here:
  http://bit.ly/ROZkdN.
- **Website:** Whether it's just for self-promotion or a
  full-blown webstore, any costs related to designing or
  maintaining (hosting and updating) your site are fully
  deductible.

ARTIST-SPECIFIC HOTSPOTS

So now that you have a sense of the general deductions you can take
advantage of, I thought it would be worthwhile to hit on a few artist-
specific hotspots and discuss when and how these kinds of expenses can
(or can't) be written off.

- **Agent Fees:** Whatever percentage your agent takes out
  for adding value to your career will be deducted from
  your income before figuring out how much tax you owe.
- **Audition Expenses:** Audition fees, trips to audition,
  submission fees, costs of recording, accompanists, and

any other related costs are all fully deductible to you in the year you paid for them.

- **Costumes:** Only if they are for performance only. Which means you wouldn't be able to wear them on the street. Clothing for auditions? Gala nights? Big meetings? No. Not if it resembles (or is) clothing that you would otherwise wear in your life. A gigantic robot costume you had to buy for a commercial or an elephant suit that you bought for a music video? Sure.

- **Framing:** Stretching, materials, the whole ball of wax.

- **Gym Memberships:** For actors, models, and the like, the issue of gym memberships is one that resurfaces again and again. Not without cause—it's a rather tricky point. The answer is sometimes yes and sometimes no. Were you required to hit the gym in order to secure a part? So much so that someone (a director,

Figure 4-3

a producer) would write a note reflecting that? Then yes. Your agent told you to lose 15? No. You just need to "keep in shape," or "look like my headshots," or "look good on stage?" Sorry, no. The working out has to be *directly* and not indirectly related to you making a specific amount of money.

- **Headshots:** Both the initial shoot and any subsequent reprints. And you should write off the cost of mailing them around under "Postage" or "Shipping."

- **Makeup:** Only if it is makeup for performance only. If this is also your street makeup, then no. Do you use the same kinds of product onstage as you do in your normal life? If so, then be sure to keep separate makeup kits so you can prove to anyone that you know which expenses you are writing off when it comes to your business.

- **Modeling Fees:** Payments to models for your photography sessions, clothing design fittings, and so forth will be deductible against any money you earn from those gigs.

- **Music for Research:** Purchasing music for research for a role, for a theme, for a piece, and so forth, can all be deducted. This is a highly underutilized area in my opinion, because if you wanted to make the argument, you could say that almost all the music you listen to is somehow influencing your art. But you have to be willing to back up that claim somehow. That takes work. Work that results in some real savings on your taxes.

- **Portfolio Costs:** The costs of both assembling and updating your portfolio and the cost of distributing it around. For many people, this is becoming a big part of their online presence, but if you're doing it old school, it can be a costly effort. And fully deductible.

- **Tickets for Research:** Another potentially underutilized deduction. Tickets to shows, galleries, openings, concerts, and the like are all deductible as research as well. Remember to save ticket stubs—and to be able to explain what you were researching or how it was connected to the work you are doing.

FIVE BIGGEST DEDUCTION MYTHS DEBUNKED

So let's pull the gloves off and address the five most frequently perpetuated myths as heard in our offices and among our clients. Maybe you've heard one or two yourself. Maybe you're one of the people keeping these myths alive. Time to set things straight on the record.

Figure 4-4

1. **If I'm not making a lot of money I can't write off all my expenses.** It won't last forever, but you have at least five years of being able to show more deductions than income before the IRS will come in and declare you a hobby. The fact is that many businesses, whether they are a craft brewery or an actor or a Silicon Valley dot com, lose money for the first couple of years. Don't be afraid to claim every deduction you are entitled to.

2. **When I work for nonprofits, I can write off my services.** This is sadly one of the biggest myths I encounter, and one that is perpetuated by nonprofits coast to coast. As a service provider, you are not able to write off work that you do "pro bono" for nonprofits. They will try to tell you that it's deductible. And that they can write you a donation letter. And that the other guy before you used to. It doesn't matter. There are many people out there doing this wrong, and they will eventually get caught. The problem is there is little way for the IRS to police the value of your time—and it's just not in their business to do so. So instead, they just say that if you donate time or services, it's just out of the goodness of your heart. Now, if you buy $20 of gas to get there, or buy $6 in office supplies to do the work, you may certainly write that off. Just like for any other client.

3. **If my _____ [cast member, coworker, etc.] _____ [pays quarterly estimates, is an LLC, etc.] I should as well.** There is a danger in assuming that you are in the same boat as the person sitting next to you in the dressing room/green room/café/studio/gallery. The danger is that even if the two of you are getting paid the exact same amount for exactly the same work, you may be in very different situations. You don't know if that person is a trust-fund baby; or has five kids, or a grandparent he supports, or a million-dollar investment portfolio. Any of those things or a hundred others could drastically alter the right course of action for him. So while you should listen attentively, don't assume

you're not doing what you're supposed to just because your neighbor is doing things differently.

4. **Managing the "business" stuff is always going to be really difficult.** Just like anything, including the first time you tried some not-even-that-fast chord changes, thinking about and tracking and dealing with your "business" is easier than it seems at first. In time you will learn the ropes, master them, and be able to navigate them effortlessly. I promise. In fact, if you are fortunate enough to build a long and stable career for yourself as a creative professional, then you will reach a point where the "business side" of what you do begins to add clarity to and inform the rest of your career in ways you'd never imagine.

5. **If I _____ [claim a loss for the year, deduct meals, include a home office, etc.] I will get audited.** There is a chance that someone who hasn't made a single mistake in 60 years of filing taxes will be audited. If it could happen to her, it could happen to you, and it has only a little to do with the kinds of things you deduct on your return. So while you should never make things up, I also stress with my clients often the importance of *communicating the reality of your situation*. If you communicate reality, you have no fear of an audit. You will proudly show them all the backup they want to support your valid business deductions.

THE GOLDEN RULE OF DEDUCTIONS: NEVER LOOK AT ANOTHER DEDUCTIONS LIST AGAIN

By now you should already be getting a sense of this rule from the many things I've discussed in this chapter, but I will make it perfectly clear. A long time ago, I decided that no deductions list could be complete—and furthermore it is generally annoying to have to go look something up to see if you can write it off or not. So following the "teach someone to fish" principle, I will now teach you the Golden Rule of Deductions, and you can forget about lists of deductions (at least, for the most part):

If you had to spend that money in order to make the money you made, you should write it off.

It's really that simple. You are a business. And as you are spending money, if you can say to yourself, "I had to buy this or pay for this in order to make the money I will make from this gig or job," then you should almost without exception write off that expense. Our clients typically encounter the following such deductions:

- microphone cables
- lipstick
- film
- rolled canvas
- wood glue
- and yes, even once . . . condoms

The point is, these are not items that will show up in any list of business deductions. They aren't a preprinted line on the tax return. They aren't default categories in QuickBooks. But that doesn't make them any less valid as deductions. Because you had to spend that money in order to make the money you made. And you need to deduct those costs from your art-related income before paying taxes on a penny of it.

- -

CASE STUDY

One year I worked with an opera singer who had racked up a significant number of 1099s in her first year as a freelance singer. She tried doing her own taxes in TurboTax and got a result that caused her to shriek in terror. Someone recommended she enlist the help of a CPA to review her situation and to see if there was anything she wasn't thinking of. What started out as a $9,100 tax bill was able to be worked down to $4,800 after I found $12,600 in deductions for her. What she thought she was saving in tax prep fees by doing it herself was certainly not saving her much money in the end. But more importantly, learning about the *kinds of things* that can be deductible and the Golden Rule of Deductions meant that the following year she came back . . . with over $18,000 in deductions. Lesson learned.

LINKS TO DEDUCTIONS
(IN CASE YOU DON'T TRUST THE GOLDEN RULE)

Okay. So if you don't trust yourself to the Golden Rule and you want a little more support, I'll provide you these lists as "kick-starters" to get your brain thinking along the right track. As previously alluded to, these lists are *not* exhaustive. They can be, however, a good starting point when you are looking to understand the types of things that you could conceivably write off for your business. If you'd like to request another more personalized list for your trade, drop me a note on my website: http://www.rockstarcpa.com/minding-your-business. If I get enough requests for one or another craft, I'll do my best to specialize for you. Without further ado, here are your lists:

- **Actors:**
  https://rockstarcpa.box.com/s/76d38a8e4a3ceae6b453
- **General Artists:**
  https://rockstarcpa.box.com/s/80531274cdff9d55879c
- **Bands:**
  https://rockstarcpa.box.com/s/30eb59f774fa17c2f44d
- **General Businesses:**
  https://rockstarcpa.box.com/s/64a55e9af6ef662000ff
- **Fashion Designers:**
  https://rockstarcpa.box.com/s/743f0f5fd96dab3ffee8
- **General Freelancers:**
  https://rockstarcpa.box.com/s/9448a81ecb0145e7e3c6
- **Graphic Designers:**
  https://rockstarcpa.box.com/s/e9aba52415894e1da5f3
- **Models:**
  https://rockstarcpa.box.com/s/082291db001c226d5e31
- **Musicians:**
  https://rockstarcpa.box.com/s/2763c88ead60ee079941
- **Photographers:**
  https://rockstarcpa.box.com/s/b3e9f733874c7a553aa4
- **Video Artists:**
  https://rockstarcpa.box.com/s/18135051643418d55d65

- **Visual Artists:**
  https://rockstarcpa.box.com/s/4d5275157bbf5852edc0
- **Writers:**
  https://rockstarcpa.box.com/s/d1a78a651a59bd66cf9b

Study Questions

1. What do you have to keep track of during the year?
2. What are the three kinds of meal expenses to keep track of?
3. When can you deduct clothing?
4. When can you deduct gym memberships?
5. When you do work pro bono for a nonprofit, do you get a tax break?
6. What is the Golden Rule of Tax Deductions?

Answers

1. Physical documents related to your income and expenses. But the online activity gets tracked as well: be it via a spreadsheet, an online program, or some accounting software.
2. The three kinds of meals are "networking," "working," and "travel." The first two are deductible at 50 percent and should be called "Meals and Entertainment." The last is fully deductible and should be lumped in with your travel deductions.
3. Clothing can only be deducted as a business expense if it is unwearable as normal clothing.
4. Gym memberships are only deductible if they are a direct requirement to get a certain job.
5. No. The donation of your time and services (with the exception of hard costs you incur) is not tax deductible in any way, regardless of whatever documentation the nonprofit provides you.
6. "If I had to spend that money in order to make the money I made, I should write it off."

5

Your Biggest Critic
Is No Longer Yourself

MEET THE IRS

My clients frequently end a conversation with me by saying, "I just don't want to be audited." Which is perfectly understandable and also perfectly ridiculous. Why is this understandable? Well, nobody wants to go through the pains of an audit. And to some extent, no matter how prepared

Figure 5-1

you are, it will be at least a little uncomfortable. You are talking about having the government get very up close and personal in your affairs: asking you for receipts, making you justify your expenses, and so forth. More importantly than anything else, who has time for all of that? The drain on your time is typically the most challenging part of an audit. This is made even more difficult for my clients because they are often engaged in activities that take a little extra explanation to the average auditor. Most auditors have experience reviewing a "typical" business—whatever that is. But they will often have a hard time understanding your business and will need a little hand holding as you walk them through your expenses. I'll dive into this in further detail later in this section.

But why is the concern over an audit also a bit ridiculous? One percent of all tax returns are audited. You could have perfect records and documentation for every receipt and *still* get audited. There is nothing you can do about it. So if you could wind up being one of the unlucky few who get plucked at random, should you really make decisions about what expenses to include based on your desire not to get audited? If there's no way to ensure you won't get chosen, you might as well reflect the reality of your situation.

There's a special kind of pain in my heart every time I hear a client say, "I don't know if I want to include these expenses . . . I think it will generate too much attention, and I don't want to get audited." What he or she is really saying is, "I'm concerned about this bad thing happening to me, and even though I can't really prevent it, I'd like to pay more in taxes this year anyway." Of course I'm making it sound really bad to accentuate the point, but that's essentially what is going on. Now, some of you might be thinking, "Okay, so you can never fully avoid the off chance that I get chosen at random, but there are always red flags to avoid, right?" I'll discuss some of those perceived and infamous "red flags" and let you know the reality of what's going on.

In general, it's best to know who you're up against. So I'm going to take some time this section to make you familiar with how the IRS operates, what you *should be afraid of*, and what you should *stop worrying about right now*.

WHO ARE THEY?

The Internal Revenue Service (IRS) is a branch of the Department of Treasury of the federal government. There are state-level Departments of Revenue, but they are essentially like their federal counterparts except much smaller, so for this purpose, I'll focus just on the big guys. There are roughly 100,000 people working for the IRS as of 2009,[*] and that makes them an enormous institution. This entity happens to be divided into four divisions: Large Business and International, Small Business and Self-Employed, Wage and Investment, and Tax-Exempt and Governmental. Most of the agents that you would encounter are from the Small Business and Self-Employed (SBSE) division. The IRS has suspected there is a large amount of lost tax revenue in the SBSE arena and has therefore increased the number of agents allocated to this section in recent years. Should this concern you? Of course not! You know exactly what to expect. Or you will. If you read on.

---

[*] *Workforce of Tomorrow Task Force: Final Report, August 2009*, Publication 4783 (IRS, August 2009).

The typical experience with the IRS involves dealing with a field agent. If the IRS were an army, the field agent would be the equivalent of a foot soldier. Field agents are the largest portion of the IRS by number, and are in the front lines of attack. They are typically the newest recruits to the IRS, but occasionally you will see an experienced veteran who just really loves the work in the field. But another important thing to understand about field agents is that—just like foot soldiers—they are typically carrying out orders. They are sent out to gather data: they will ask you for information, supporting documents, schedules, and so forth, and then they will write up their report and submit it to their supervisor for review. At the end of their review, you will receive a determination about any tax that is due or refund owed to you. (Yes—it is possible to have a refund be the result of an audit. They are fair about finding both the good and the bad in the process.) But is the field agent the one to complain to when you don't like the result? No. For that you go to the appeals process.

The field agent is sent out to collect data and interpret the findings within the strictest interpretation of the IRS code. There is little gray area with field agents, though you can certainly do work in educating them about *your particular business* if that is needed. But at the end of the day, if they don't see eye to eye with you, it's not the time to start the waterworks and state, "But there's just *no way* I could owe all that money . . . I mean, look at me! I'm a starving artist. Literally. I have no money for food!" The field agent won't care. It's not his or her job. The appeals process is where you can state your case and make those kind of "Let's get real" defenses. Maybe you really don't make any money doing what you do. Maybe somehow the paper trail just didn't do a good job of portraying the reality of your situation. In the appeals process, you lay out your best argument and hope for some mercy from the high-ups.

And if at *any point* in the process you find yourself not being heard, there is the taxpayer advocate office. They are a division of the IRS that is intentionally separate from all other divisions. (Hence they weren't mentioned in the earlier breakdown of hierarchy.) The taxpayer advocate is designed to jump in when there are cases of gross injustice or negligence happening on the part of the IRS. I'll give you an example to illustrate what I'm talking about.

CASE STUDY

I had one client due a significant refund on her 2010 tax return. She filed on time in March of 2011 and was hoping to get her refund sometime around April of the same year. Instead, she didn't see her money, and didn't see it, and didn't see it . . . and around May, she called me to follow up. My investigation into it resulted in the IRS sending her a letter that she was the victim of identity theft and that someone had filed a return with her social security number on it. Now they needed to investigate to determine who was the real taxpayer and who was the phony. How long would that take? "Six to eight weeks," they said. Okay. So we waited through June and July and called back in August. At that point they determined that she was in fact the true taxpayer and the other person was a fake. "Did you see where the refund was deposited?" I asked. "Yes," they said. "So you see that is not an account that my client is in possession of, correct?" I asked. "Yes," they said.

At this point I was thinking this was fairly cut and dry. They know where the money is. Where it was incorrectly sent. And they can get it back and find the bad guy and in the meantime deposit the money into my client's account. Instead I heard that it would take another six to eight weeks to track that down and get us the money. Okay. I figured we were close enough and it was worth the wait. We waited through August and September and called back in October. Nothing. Waited through October and November. Nothing. Frequent calls from my office were not effective in getting the IRS to close this investigation and refund my client her money. So I called the taxpayer advocate on her behalf. I explained to them that yes, there was a case of identity theft, and that we were reasonable about waiting until August for the refund. But the IRS had subsequently blown off two additional deadlines, and my client was undergoing some financial hardships as a result of not having this money. They took a look at the case, found the IRS to be negligent in their handling of the matter, and spurred us to a conclusion in three weeks.

That was an unfortunate series of events, but one that exemplifies cases where the taxpayer advocate can step in and come to your assistance. Not all cases work out positively in the end, but then again, most cases don't require the advocate to step in. Let's take a look at how the IRS handles most audits.

HOW DO THEY WORK?

The first (and most common) approach to a tax return is called a "correspondence audit." Harsh words, but not something worth sweating too much. This is how a correspondence audit takes place:

1. The IRS will send you a letter (this is where the correspondence comes from) and ask you for additional information supporting one or more lines on your tax return. Maybe they want to see additional information about your travel expenses. Or they would like to see the receipts for your meals and entertainment expense. You owe them that information *and nothing more.*

2. You send in your documentation and they review it. If you have done a good job tracking your receipts and can back up your expenses, it ends here. *Or,* if you have not done a good job keeping up with your responsibilities, they may proceed to a step three.

3   *If* you are not able to provide adequate support for the expenses they are reviewing, one of two things could happen. They may simply make an adjustment for the unsupported amount and tell you the deductions aren't allowed and you owe a little more tax. Or if you look *really* disorganized and in bad shape, and they have reason to believe you just made up the whole tax return, then they may decide to broaden the scope of their audit. Let's hope that you don't get to a step three. If you follow along with the ideas in this book, you'll be in good shape.

It's important to note at this point that I haven't talked about in-person meetings. No Will Ferrell showing up at your bakery like in the film *Stranger than Fiction.* Though it makes for better movies, the reality is that the IRS can't afford to send everyone out for every single audit and have them spend the time to go through everything face to face. Good news?

I think so. Correspondence audits can be dealt with on your time (as opposed to during set meeting times) and can be done in your pajamas (as opposed to in a formal setting).

In-person meetings can certainly occur. They are the first step in a very few audits: usually those that involve really complex businesses or really unusual-looking tax returns. But they can also happen as an escalation of a normal correspondence audit. That *can* happen. But as good pupils of *Minding Your Business*, that won't be you. Of course not.

And a final word on "red flags." There is no such thing as a definitive list of red flags. And in general they are not worth concerning yourself with as long as you are presenting the reality of your situation. But if you are very curious, the IRS publishes a report every year with its top twelve targets. The targets enumerated in the most recent report are:

1. **Making Too Much Money:** Returns with incomes over $200,000 have a 4 percent chance of being audited. Returns over $1 million have a 12.5 percent chance. Compared with 1 percent for returns under $200,000, those making more money are far more likely to be audited. But do I discourage making money? Absolutely not.

2. **Not Reporting Income:** Since the IRS gets copies of every 1099 and W2 generated with your social security number on it, not reporting that money is likely to cause at least a basic correspondence audit to clear things up. In fact, let's assume it's a guarantee.

3. **Large Amounts of Charitable Contributions:** Amounts under $500 are not required to provide much additional information, but beyond that, be sure to include all supporting information with your deductions. Should you shy away from donating? Absolutely not. Just keep track of those records.

4. **Home Offices:** This does not mean you shouldn't claim the home office that you actually use regularly and exclusively for your work. But taking an unreasonably high percentage or throwing in expenses that are entirely for personal purposes will draw some attention.

5. **Deducting Real Estate Losses:** A couple or individual owning and actively managing one rental property can deduct up to $25,000 in losses against their other income. But if you are trying to claim infinite losses under the guise of being a "real estate professional," be sure you can back up the time you spend during the year on your properties—i.e., if you have another full-time job reported, it'll be tough to argue you spend more than 50 percent of your working hours in real estate.

6. **Travel, Meals, and Entertainment:** Again, not something you want to avoid reporting just for fear of scrutiny. But if these expenses make up an unusually high percentage of your expenses, you may want to think about how you are spending your money during the year. Very few business models involve spending the majority of your money on food and drinks (that you aren't turning around and selling).

7. **100 Percent Business Use of a Vehicle:** If you don't have another car or bicycle and don't live by any trains or buses, be prepared to explain how your legs are your only form of personal transportation. Or keep meticulous record of your business driving. Or just be realistic about the percentage of business use.

8. **Writing Off a Loss from a Hobby:** You learned a while back in this book why this isn't allowed. And if you lose track of years and end up blowing the Five-Year Rule, be sure that the IRS will write you a letter back adjusting your numbers to remove the loss.

9. **Cash Businesses:** Ever been tempted to see what's behind door number three? The IRS is equally curious about that which they cannot track, and cash businesses are exactly that—difficult to track. With very little paper trail, they provide the *opportunity* for deception. These types of businesses tend to draw a little more attention.

10. **Foreign Bank Accounts:** If you are flashy or conniving enough to be running money through foreign bank accounts and not reporting it . . . well, you kind of deserve to be audited, don't you?

11. **Currency Exchanges:** Businesses that involve changing out large sums of cash (e.g., casinos) are great targets for the IRS. These transactions are often linked to other fraudulent or illegal behavior, and other government agencies have put the pressure on the IRS to tip them off.

12. **Unusually High Deductions:** Some years you have to spend or invest a lot of your money. But if you consistently have deductions that eat away almost *all* of your income, it begs the question, "Well how does this person survive? How do they buy bread? Or pay rent?" If there's a valid answer to these questions, such as "My girlfriend pays for everything" or "I've racked up $10,000 in credit card debt this year," then no worries. But if you are adding deductions that don't really belong, then you have a problem.

WHY SHOULD I CARE?

Okay. You get a sense of who the IRS is and how they operate, but why does this matter? Why should you care? Because at the end of the day, they are your worst-case scenario. If everything takes a turn for the worst, you may end up needing to deal with them, and there is a good way and a bad way of approaching it. I'll discuss some best practices in a moment, but for now, I want to give you a little more background on the kinds of things you may see from the IRS and how they may impact your taxes.

A correspondence audit may ask you for additional information about one or another deduction you were trying to claim. And hopefully you have the documentation to back that up. But that's not even the most common kind of letter you receive from the IRS. The average letter from the IRS (see fig. 5-2) is just a request for something they don't have. This example involved someone who failed to include some stock sales on their return. Did they actually owe all the taxes indicated in the letter? No. Because the IRS only knew how much they sold the stock for. They didn't know that the stocks were actually sold at a loss. The issue was resolved with no additional tax due. In order to scare you into action (because we are so inundated with paper mail, and most of it is junk mail anyway), they tend to get aggressive with the language in these

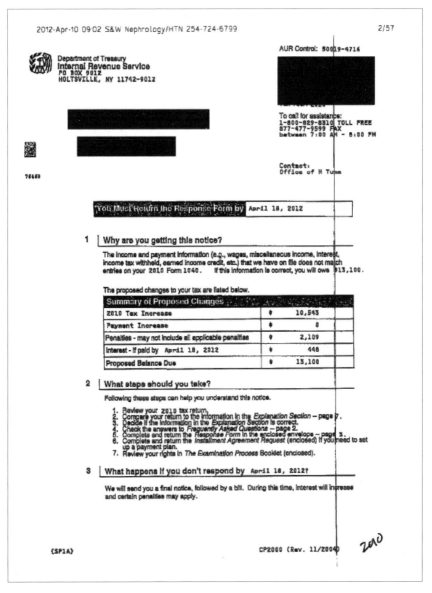

Figure 5-2

simple requests. It's not uncommon to see something like *Final Notice* on the first letter you get from them. Is this 100 percent accurate? No. But again, they are just trying to kick-start you into action. Another common letter tactic is to tell you that you owe them $X,XXX in additional taxes because you didn't (fill in the blank). This is again typically the result of some missing information—*not* the result of you actually doing anything wrong. The moral of the story?

The first thing you should do when you get any *kind of letter from the IRS is to take a breath, calm down, and try to get to the bottom of what they are asking you.*

It will be difficult to avoid panic. The language they use will be pushing you into what may feel like an anxiety attack. But don't give in to this. Odds are pretty good that there is a simple solution. You just have to find out what they are looking for and get it in their hands as soon as possible. Here's another important note:

If you can't figure out what the letter is asking you for, seek out some help.

Many accountants will interpret a letter for you free of charge. But even if you have to pay someone for an hour of his or her time to get a sense of what you need to do, it will be well worth it. I had a client come to me one year with a paper grocery bag full of unopened letters from the IRS. Yes, I said unopened. There was one letter opened, and she hadn't been able to interpret it on her own, so she'd just stopped opening them. And she didn't take action on this until they froze her accounts. Zip to the end of the story: she did owe a couple thousand dollars in taxes from some returns she didn't file. But the interest and penalties involved for not dealing with it in a timely manner added a couple thousand more to her balance due. Some of it was unavoidable. But some of it was most certainly avoidable and just the resulting of not addressing things in a timely manner.

HOW TO MAKE THE IRS YOUR FRIEND (AND WHY YOU SHOULD)

Let's talk about how to make the IRS your friend—and why that's a worthwhile endeavor. There's really only two options here: you can play along with the rules, or you can ignore your responsibilities and try to not get caught. But the IRS can be in many cases a pretty understanding bunch. It's all about communication. You need to know how to communicate with them, how to present yourself and your information, and how to stand behind your deductions.

I have had clients approach me who decide for one reason or another that they will ignore the IRS for a long time—in some cases, for years at a time. The reasons are varied: some clients admit to holding out hope that if they just wait long enough, the IRS will give up on them and move along; others didn't have the financial means to address whatever problem was coming up; and still others didn't know how to begin and got frustrated. If you are one of those who have tried to ignore the IRS for a while, you know firsthand that there is no escaping a situation once you are on their radar. Rather, things will quickly accelerate and take a turn for the worse. What might have started out as a simple problem (e.g., they are just missing a document that you had sent to them, which got lost in the mail) can quickly escalate to several nasty letters, followed by the assumption of balances due, and eventually a levy against your bank accounts and a lien against your future earnings. They do this because they fear that you are attempting to escape without ever dealing with the situation. How would they know anything to the contrary? You haven't let them know what's going on. If you just don't have the financial means to address a balance due, again, some simple communication can smooth things out. If you've ever owed some money to the federal government for student loans, you understand that letting them know about your financial situation can often result in either reduced payments or even a temporary forbearance (period of not paying). The IRS is no different. They are willing to work with you in whatever situation you find yourself.

So let's talk about a few best practices when dealing with the IRS.

1. **Communicate quickly and often.** The IRS doesn't use e-mail. Ever. So you'll be relegated to the world of paper mail and fax machines. You can talk on the phone as well, which isn't a bad thing to do, but there's less of a paper trail—which the IRS loves to see. So if you ever see a notice from the IRS, you need to communicate with them directly and right away. Include a copy of the notice you received, and let them know you are working on a solution for them. That's the first letter you drop in the mail, and you send it as soon as you get their notice. Then, you keep communicating by letter or fax as often as you need to until you get the matter figured out.

2. **Present your information as if you were participating in a debate.** Lay out the request they made (again including copies of anything they sent you), and step by step begin to work toward a solution.

For example, if they are asking you for some missing information from your return, you provide them the original notice and an outline of the two or three things they asked for, and then subsequent pages will have the supporting information. Make it easy for them (or your neighbor) to understand how you are providing the information in full. If you don't know how to get a hold of what they want, you need to ask for help. Talk to an accountant or visit your local IRS office.

3. **Make your deductions easy for the IRS to understand.** Yes, artists and creatives are allowed to deduct a great many things that the average taxpayer cannot. If you are in the film industry, for example, you might be able to write off your movie tickets as research. Do yourself a favor and call these "research" in your documentation as opposed to "movie tickets." You don't have the benefit of having a long, drawn-out conversation with them each step of the way, so being clear and concise is important.

4. **Ask for clarification of things you don't understand.** If you don't have a good working relationship with an accountant, and you can't make it to a local IRS office in the near future, it's acceptable to write back just asking for clarification on a letter you receive. The notices and letters cranked out by the IRS are spit out by computers and have little in the way of a "personal touch." Writing your letter seeking clarification will garner you a response that is written by an actual human and will hopefully resolve some of those questions you have. *And* you will also get credit for a quick response—which *does* get noted on your account. You get "credit" for doing the right thing when it comes to the IRS. Nobody will ever talk about this, and it's not something I can explain or quantify for you, but in my experience, the IRS is much easier to work with when the client is open and freely communicating. It's just the way it is. Think of it this way: you could either be the victim

of many frequent communications from the IRS, *or* you could be proactive and make them the victim of your overcommunicating. Don't be the victim—get proactive and take control of the situation.

WHAT TO DO IF YOU END UP FACING OFF

Let's imagine that things get difficult. You received your letter, communicated often, and sent back the information you thought they needed, and they still want to go head to head on a few points. It's time to come face to face with the IRS. Here's how you're going to make this go as smoothly as possible for yourself.

You will want to ask for as much time as you need to prepare. You can make this request in writing or by calling the field agent assigned to your case (at this point, there would be one local agent who is identified on the letters you receive). Let the agent know that you have received his or her letter, and that you are putting together the information he or she requested and need some time. Asking for a few weeks or even a couple of months is not unusual. But don't push it too far—everyone likes to get things off their to-do list, and the IRS is no different. Your case is "open" until it's "closed" with them, and until that point, you will need to stay in constant communication with them in order to avoid angering anybody. If you are working with an accountant to assist you in this process, let the IRS know you have found someone to help you out, and they need time to review your documentation and help you put things together.

When should you deal with the IRS directly, and when should you get some help? Not every audit requires the intervention of a CPA. But if you are unclear about what the IRS is asking for or how to best defend yourself, getting help is not a bad idea. It might cost you some money to get the help you need, but you could wind up saving yourself hundreds or thousands of dollars in the process. A good CPA knows how to "talk the talk" that the IRS is looking for, and can act as a valuable translator when trying to parlay your deductions into common business-speak. If you retain the services of a CPA, you will most likely sign over a limited power of attorney that will grant him or her the ability to discuss these matters with the IRS on your behalf. On the other hand, there are the cases where the IRS wants documentation of your $3,232 in travel expenses for the year, and being the amazing student of *Minding Your Business* that you are, you are ready to hand over the documentation that accounts for all of that spending. Go ahead and DIY. Just be careful to avoid opening up new areas of inquiry. If all they want is travel, just give them travel. There's no need to start talking about your meals and entertainment expenses or asking the question you have about research deductions. There will be a better place and time for that to come.

Make sure to document everything. Have a file, a document, a notebook, an anything, where you write down your timeline. This will become very important, especially if things are taking an unfairly long time to get resolved. You will want to know everything that has transpired and when. So your log (see fig. 5-3) will have every letter you received, every phone call you placed, every letter you sent, the nature of what was said, and the name and ID number of the agent involved. When you call, you will get a different agent every time, so it's important to know who said what at the end of the day. Keep your log, along with copies of everything you send and receive, in a safe place. This is your ammunition in battle.

Date	Type of Communication (letter, phone call, etc)	Agent Name	ID Number	Notes:
02/12/11	Letter	Jones	1112022	Letter requested additional info about travel deductions
02/20/11	Phone call	Smith	1113033	Called to clarify what they need, just send itineraries

Figure 5-3

If you show them everything you have and they still aren't satisfied, or if you legitimately have a balance due, it's best to deal with it as quickly as possible, because taxes are something that recur every year. Getting behind on one year and not catching up quickly *can* lead to a perpetual cycle where you're never fully caught up. At the same time, it's important to know that owing money to the IRS is not going to cost you an arm and a leg. Penalties and interest for not filing on time or not communicating properly—those can add up quickly. But once a balance due is established, the interest rates once you are making payments is rather low. It's cheaper than almost any other money you can borrow, so if you have to decide between paying down your credit card bill or paying the IRS in one big chunk, pay down the credit card and take your time with the IRS.

A word on offers in compromise. The offer in compromise (OIC) system was put into place by the IRS sometime back in order to give people negotiating power when dealing with a large balance they could never repay in the near future. I had a client, for example, that owed a little more than $20,000 from one year and had lost her job, couldn't demonstrate much income at all right now, and had no liquid assets she could turn into cash to pay the bill. I put in an offer for her of a little more than $5,000 in money she could scrape together, and the IRS settled her debt for the amount I offered. Lately, an onslaught of late-night TV accounting firms have taken the OIC system to an unfortunate place of taking advantage of people. The attorneys general of many states (including my home state of Illinois) have cracked down on their deceitful practices and in some cases have thrown these people in jail. Here's what you need to know:

- The IRS is not really in a place where they need to make deals right now. Even as recently as the year 2000, many more deals were being accepted at a much greater savings to the taxpayer. But these days, the IRS is much more interested in holding on to that IOU and letting you take as long as you need to pay it off.
- In order to make a deal stick, you need to come up with a substantial amount of money *right now*. The deal doesn't stretch over a long period of time. You are giving them a big percentage of the money today in exchange for them writing the rest of it off as uncollectible.
- Which brings us to the third point: you need to demonstrate a lack of "collectability" in the near future. Which is why an OIC is so unlikely for most people. You have to have been making enough to have a pretty sizable tax bill right now, *and* have enough in your pocket to pay a big chunk of it, but have (little to) no determinable income in the near future to make payments over time. If this perfect storm seems unlikely or uncommon, you're correct. Which is why you need to take the advice of a trusted accountant or advisor before paying someone to

help you put an offer together. If you are going to use a tax debt relief firm, ask them for *recent* statistics about the offers they have submitted, and ask to speak to those clients they were successful with. Try to obtain an honest assessment of your offer and its chances.

Study Questions

1. What percentage of tax returns are audited?
2. Should you worry about getting audited?
3. What's the first thing to do if you receive a letter from the IRS?
4. What four things are key to making the IRS fall in love with you?
5. If you owe a substantial amount of taxes, do you have a good chance to settle for pennies on the dollar?

Answers

1. About 1 percent of tax returns are audited every year.
2. Absolutely not. Not when you are doing a good job of presenting the reality of your situation.
3. Take a breath, calm down, and try to figure out what they are asking of you.
4. Communicate quickly and often, lay out your responses in an organized way, translate your deductions to something they can understand, and ask for clarification when you don't understand something.
5. No, the IRS isn't much in the business of settling anymore. The best course of action is to enter into an installment agreement to get you back in "good status" with the government.

6

Parting Thoughts

YOUR "TEAM"

Getting good advice is critical at any major junction in your life. And going into business for yourself is no exception. Hopefully over time you'll be able to build up a team to handle many of the things you won't have time to pay attention to yourself. These people could include:

- A bookkeeper to keep track of your income and expenses for you so that you can spend more time focusing on your projects, your clients, your new songs, and so forth.
- A publicist who will get your amazing work noticed by the print publications, radio, and TV.
- An attorney to help navigate contracts, settle any intellectual property disputes, and so forth.
- An office manager to make phone calls for you, schedule appointments, and so forth.
- Any number of other qualified people to back-fill your operations.

The important thing to consider here is what your time will be best spent doing. Odds are good that there are a lot of parts of your operation that you won't be good at—and that's perfectly normal. You can't worry about being good at everything, because very, very few people are. And it's usually not worth their time to do everything themselves anyway. So you focus on what you can do best and leave the rest to specialists.

That said, it's rare that you get to hit the ground running with a full team in place to support you. If you are in such a position, count yourself fortunate. But for the rest of you, you may easily find yourself wearing the many and varied hats of a small business owner. In fact, it's probably a good thing that you are doing a number of these things yourself at first. It will teach you what it takes to get the job done and make you better suited to know what to expect and how to manage other people when they start doing the work for you. Take the example of two talented film directors. The first spent years trying to promote her own career: taking meetings all over the country, building up an impressive reel, networking with others in the industry, managing her online reputation . . . And eventually she reached a level of success where someone else wanted to help land her some really great projects. Then let's look at another equally talented director whose first major project was a big hit, and he was approached by a rep from LA who wanted to help run his career and get him new work. Who will be better suited to know when the rep is not doing his or her job? How to guide the rep in getting projects that the director is really interested in working on?

Even if you are doing the majority of the work yourself, it's important to get a few key people in place from the beginning. Let's meet the players on your team.

WHO ARE THE PLAYERS?

Figure 6-1

These initial members of your "team" aren't necessarily people you will have on payroll right away. You may not even use them on a regular basis. It's more important to find them and develop a good working relationship with them. Have them "on call" so that when situations come up that need attention, you know exactly who can help. The last thing you want to be doing when an urgent contract dispute arises is thumbing through the phone book for attorneys in your city. So who are the key players on your team?

- **A CPA:** (I will disclose and admit a healthy amount of bias here. Being a certified public accountant myself, I know what it takes and what the designation will guarantee you as a client. If you're curious, search online for the "value of using a CPA" and you will find a number of excellent explanations.) The CPA needs to be a part of an initial conversation about how to set up your business legally: sole proprietorship, corporation, LLC, and so forth. But what else do you want to contact him or her about?
  - How do you pay yourself?
  - What kinds of records should you be keeping about your income and expenses?
  - What are industry practices in terms of getting paid by your clients?
  - How do you deal with sales taxes?
  - What happens if you do work or earn money in several different states?
  - What is the best way for you to "hire" additional help?
  - How much do you need to set aside for taxes?

- **An Attorney:** The attorney will also be a part of the initial conversation about which form of business is right for you. And you may even have him or her draft your articles of incorporation or a partnership agreement as necessary. But what else might an attorney be able to help you with?
  - Setting up a template contract for services

performed that you can reuse with all of your
clients.

o Knowing what—if anything—you should think
about trademarking or copywriting.

o Knowing what risks you are facing by engaging in
the line of business you are in.

o Discussing how to protect your personal assets from
your professional activities.

o (Plus, it's always nice to know you have an attorney.
It's comforting just to say that out loud.)

- **A Banker:** This one might not be as obvious to most
people, but I want to make a strong argument for it. In
this day and age, you generally have two options when
you look at banking: go big or go small. The big banks
will offer you the following: nationwide access, amazing
online and mobile tools, and almost every other ease and
convenience you could imagine. The smaller community
banks will offer something else: a personal connection.
Whether you choose to go big or small—and especially if
you choose to go big—starting a relationship with a business banker at a local branch can prove invaluable in the
future. Example number one? It takes but one try waiting through hold on the national phone lines talking to a
service rep who doesn't know you and is not particularly
motivated to come to your service before you realize how
much nicer it would be to call the man or woman down
the street who *knows you* and is willing to go to bat for you.
Example two? Let's say it's three years later and it's time
for you to buy some new cameras, a new truck, a trailer for
your gear so you can actually stretch out in the van . . . Do
you want to blindly submit an application online, or go to
someone who understands your business and where you
came from and can help you position yourself to look as
strong as possible? I think we all know the answer to
this one.

HOW TO PULL THEM TOGETHER

Now that you know the targets on the list, let's talk about a few considerations in putting the team together. There's no recommended order of assembly, so start wherever you are comfortable. If you already have a good relationship with your current bank, you could start with a business banker at that bank and move on from there. But however you get started, it's important to have a few things in mind as you build your team and to have a few key questions to ask them when you get started.

Ways to locate the right person:

1. **Personal Referrals:** This is always the best way to get a hold of *any* service provider, whether it's a dentist or a plumber or an attorney. Ask around, post on Facebook, call your family, find out who the people *you know and trust* are already using. Odds are they will be a good fit for you as well. Just be mindful that you are looking for someone with experience in *your particular area*, so not every referral will be on your list of candidates.

2. **Business Referrals:** Another good way to find good people. It's the spiderweb approach. Start by finding a good banker. Ask the banker what CPAs and attorneys he or she recommends. All business advisers take their reputations very seriously, and part of that reputation is the names they pass on to others, so you're not likely to get a bad name that way. Again, just be mindful of the industry expertise they will need.

3. **Online Searches:** There are now targeted online profile searches for providers of almost any kind. For those of you starting creative businesses, you could focus on these to get started (if you have no referrals or anything else to use):

   • http://www.nolo.com/legal-encyclopedia/find-lawyer-how-to-find-attorney-29868.html
   • http://lawyers.findlaw.com/?DCMP=GOO-DIR_LawyerGenExp-HowTo&HBX_PK=how+to+find+a+lawyer

- http://www.cpadirectory.com/
- http://www.bookkeepinghelp.com/

Questions to ask:

1. What kind of credentials do you hold, and for how long have you held them?
2. What experience do you have working with (insert your trade here)? Get as specific as possible.
3. How will you charge me for your services?
4. What will I receive for my money? Once you start talking about money, talk about deliverables. You know what you need to deliver to your fans, clients, and so forth in exchange for their money. What are you getting for yours?
5. What are your policies about communication? How long does it typically take for you to _____?
6. Whom at your firm will I be working with? Get a sense of what kind of work will be done with the partner or individual directly and what work he or she assigns to lower-level staff.
7. Are you available to me year round? Many accountants and attorneys like to work hard for a part of the year and take some extended time off at other points. Make sure that you have someone (at least a fallback contact) available to you year round. You never know when you'll need to call . . .
8. Ask to speak to one or two clients that are similar to you. Many professionals are protective of their clients and their clients' privacy, so don't be surprised if they need time to clear this with the client first. (You'll appreciate that same discretion when you become their client.) But every good service provider should be able to put you in contact with at least *one* current client that has similar needs to you.
9. What can I do to help the process and minimize your fees going forward?
10. And lastly, throw in some questions to get a sense of his or her personality. You'll be surprised how important this

is for a good fit. He or she doesn't need to become your best friend, but you will want someone that you'll see as a teammate and ally. It's the only way to keep all this enjoyable.

WHEN IS DIY OKAY?

The DIY movement is huge in almost every aspect of life. Maybe instead of going to the doctor, you find yourself Googling your symptoms to find some home remedies. Or maybe instead of having a professional show you how to improve your Photoshop® skills, you start YouTubing some tutorial videos. Making business decisions and thinking about taxes is no different. And the DIY options out there are plentiful.

First, let's look at the business setup process. You have received in this book alone a great wealth of information about the different forms of business, and hopefully have some good ideas about not only where you ought to be right now but also where you would like your career path to take you. That said, nothing compares to sitting down with a professional to review *your specific circumstances*. Why? Numbers are numbers, charts are meant as guidelines, and every single one of you reading this book comes from a different financial background. Some are more numbers-savvy than others. Some may naturally be more organized than others. And some (don't rush to judgment) may have money from other sources. All of these factors can play a profound role in determining the best form of business for someone.

If, however, you do your homework—and you've not only read this book but have gotten several other opinions and synthesized them into the best possible course of action for you—then you're a decent candidate for DIY incorporation. And that's easy enough. Searching for the term *incorporation* will land you thousands of results. Go with someone reputable (think first page of results), and skip all the add-ons. You can act as your own registered agent, at your own address, and you don't need the corporate seal or corporate book (glorified binder). Make these things yourself, and save the money for your business.

What about bookkeeping? This one can hands down be done by yourself. Until you get to a level of activity where keeping up with your income and expenses on a monthly basis becomes overwhelming, you can absolutely keep track of things yourself. Many of the tools discussed earlier in the book are designed with the nonaccountant in mind, and though they may not be marvels of modern user-experience design, they will get the job done. When should you start thinking about hiring someone else? Here's a simple equation:

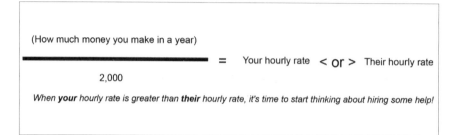

(How much money you make in a year)

$$\frac{\text{(How much money you make in a year)}}{2,000} = \text{Your hourly rate} \quad < \text{or} > \quad \text{Their hourly rate}$$

*When **your** hourly rate is greater than **their** hourly rate, it's time to start thinking about hiring some help!*

Figure 6-2

And last (but certainly not least), there's your tax return. So when is it appropriate to do your own tax return? Most "employees" can handle filing their own taxes. Mortgages, W2s, and so forth are easily handled by most tax preparation software. The exception here are "employee type" creatives who have a significant number of work-related expenses, or who have to file returns in many states. Those are issues best left to a professional. Now comes the more challenging statement.

If you are self-employed or have an incorporated business of some kind, having a professional do your taxes will pay off. Ninety-nine percent of the time. Often enough that it's fair to say unequivocally. Why? Let's start with the issue of time and money. You make money doing what you do best. Sculpting. Crafting. Writing. Surveying society and exploring what it means to be human. CPAs and other tax preparers make money doing what they do best. This is not a flagrant plug of Adam Smith—more a plea to think honestly about the best use of your time. It will take the average tax preparer *far* less time than you to do the return, and in the process (if he or she is doing a good job), he or she will provide you with tips and advice to make your life even easier over the course of the coming year. Secondly, most tax software is driven by interview format: questions and answers. But the challenge (especially as it pertains to creative and artistic folk) is that it might not know the right questions to ask you. And how would you know the difference? The most common unfortunate result of not asking the right questions is that the taxpayer ends up overpaying. So are you really saving money by using that online program?

Enough of the soapbox. If you end up going DIY anyway, consider having a professional review the return every once in a while. Maybe every three years. Don't be surprised if you are asked to pay a fee as if he or she were preparing the return from scratch—that's the only way to truly validate your numbers. But it might be worth it just to know that you didn't miss anything, that there's no changes you weren't aware of, and most importantly, that you're not paying more in taxes than you need to.

MINDING YOUR RESPONSIBILITIES

So I've talked a lot about a number of considerations as you get your creative career launched, such as:

1. Deciding if you qualify as a business or a hobby.
2. Getting paid as a contractor versus as an employee.
3. Deciding whether to be self-employed or incorporate.
4. Choosing the right form of incorporation.

And I've talked about a number of things you need to keep track of along the way, such as:

1. Tracking income from various sources.
2. Having a record of your expenses sorted by category.
3. Interacting with your team.
4. Planning for upcoming tax bills.

Now, how exactly do you put this all together while still having time to focus on what counts for you? The first thing to remember is that what at first seems like a daunting task will become easier and easier as you become more familiar with the processes. If you remember the first time you tried to edit a manuscript, or the first time you had to actually arrange and write down parts for supporting musicians, or code a flash website animation, it probably seemed like a feat that would take divine intervention to accomplish. But with each notch in your belt, the time it took to get the process going and execute your vision decreased. So much so that at this point, many of those once daunting tasks are just a part of your everyday operations. The same can be true with paying attention to your money. Keep up with it regularly, and you will find it becoming second nature. Leave it a once-a-year all-nighter operation and it is likely going to challenge you year after year.

Key Point

Keep up with your income and expenses regularly, and this will all become second nature to you—just like anything else.

Why is this important? Because my goal here is not to burden you with unnecessary work throughout the year. It's about building strong habits that will carry you through the various stages of your career. And that's exactly what you can expect if you use the tips and tricks in this book. Let's review the key ongoing responsibilities you've got throughout the year and help you set the reminders you need to make it all work like clockwork.

Tracking Income from Various Sources

If you are self-employed, you will have the added benefit of one (or several) 1099s coming at you each January that will verify the amount of income you received from your vendors. But you've got to treat it as just that—a verification—and not a conclusive source. For better or worse, the kinds of agencies and organizations that tend to employ creatives can struggle sometimes in keeping accurate records themselves, and every tax season, I have more than a handful of clients who end up with discrepancies with the 1099s they received. *Significant* discrepancies that might have cost them thousands in extra taxes paid. Do your own tracking, whether it's by simple spreadsheet or a basic accounting system. For those of you who are incorporated in some form, it will be mandatory for you to track your own income. Having that separate business bank account can help with this, as the total deposits for the year are going to roughly equate to your business income. But due to timing differences, this isn't always perfect. It's best to keep your own record and use the bank statement as a backup. And here's another important note:

Key Point

Bank statements don't last forever. Save them on your computer or another source for backup.

As a certified B-corporation, we at Rockstar CPA love being paperless. But at year end, the bank will often only provide the last four to six months of transactions online. It's worth saving them as you go to make sure you've got complete records.

Recording Expenses by Category

Again, whether you are self-employed or incorporated, a separate bank account will do *wonders* in helping you not miss a deduction along the way. So track every transaction in and out of this account, and tag them each with a category of expense. The categorization isn't incredibly important, as long as it's something that means something to you and something you can communicate to your tax preparer at year end. He or she will be able to help you characterize it in a way that makes sense to the IRS. How often do you need to update your records? Use this as a guide: however long it takes you to get up to date in two hours. If you can work through a whole month's worth of activity in two hours, then you can save it for a monthly activity. If you do enough business that you generate two hours' worth of data in a week, then set this as a weekly task in your calendar.

Interacting with Your Team

How often should you circle the wagons with your team? Depends on your needs. But your accountant should require the most contact throughout the year. At least on a quarterly basis, you should update your CPA with your income and expenses to date. It's also a good opportunity for your accountant to pass on any new laws or changes to how you should be doing things going forward. In some cases, a more thorough midyear planning session can be helpful, especially if you are responsible for planning for the majority of your tax payments during the year. The attorney should be contacted more as you first get started and then less frequently as you become familiar with the documents you see on a regular basis. You should also be able to reuse many of the contract templates he or she helps you set up. The banker will also be accessed on an as-needed basis, but it's not a bad idea to meet up and grab a coffee with him or her once a quarter. Keep your banker posted on your business progress and your ideas for the future. It will help develop a sense of your trustworthiness, which can affect how strongly he or she goes to bat for you when you need a loan. It's also a good excuse to remind him or her of who you are and what you look like—all the more important in an era where you're depositing checks by smartphone.

Planning for Your Tax Payments

This one will depend a lot on how you are set up—although you will generally need to review your situation once a quarter regardless. If you're in a position where you need to send in quarterly payments (in the form of individual estimated payments or business payroll tax payments), then how your business is doing will impact the size of those payments. This one really brings it all together. Your income tracking leads you to your overall income figure, the expense tracking leads you to a sense of your deductions, your CPA will advise you about your potential tax liability, and you adjust your savings along the way to plan for the payments you need to make. It looks kind of like this:

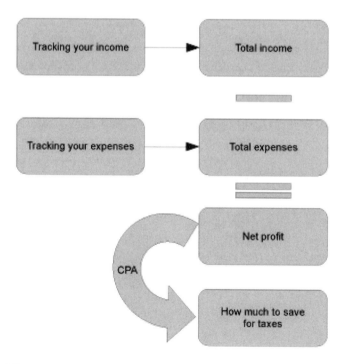

Figure 6-3

WHAT TO IGNORE IN THE
[DRESSING ROOM/GREEN ROOM/CAFÉ/GALLERY]

Figure 6-4

It's difficult to ignore the chatter. Creative individuals tend to operate in really supportive communities. It's one way that you can fight the challenges of making money, the constant desire to unlock the beauty in the world, the parents not understanding your choices, and so forth. And you may be tempted to work together to solve your tax issues, just like you may brainstorm options for how to promote your next show. This can be a rather dangerous impulse.

The danger lies in the *extremely* personal nature of one's income taxes. You may be sitting in a dressing room, next to five other actors or actresses who you *know* are all getting paid the exact same amount as you are for exactly the same amount of time. Maybe it's even the only gig that each of you will work on in a year. Unfortunately, there are so many factors impacting your individual tax returns, it's impossible to assume that the same course of action will serve each of you sufficiently. Here are a few things that people tend to overhear and misapply to their lives:

- **Estimated Payments:** This has to be the No. 1 mistaken assumption from green-room chatter. It's nobody's fault—it would make good sense that if two people were on the same kind of contract and one were making estimated payments (or "filing quarterly," as it's often misleadingly referred to), the other should as well. There is simply *no way* of knowing what else is impacting that person's individual taxes that makes them have to pay estimated taxes. Being married to a wage earner, having other sources of residual income, owning your home, having rental properties—these are all things that could impact whether someone is required to file quarterly or not. Does that mean you should ignore it entirely? Absolutely not. Just drop your tax professional a line, and find out if you have anything to worry about.

- **Deductibility of Expenses:** Again, it would make sense that something deductible for one member of a band would be deductible to another. And while this is usually the case, it can certainly come about that something is deductible for one person but not for another. Need an example? Okay. Both the drummer and the bassist of a band buy a new laptop in the same year. The drummer uses his laptop to search for new gigs, book dates for the band, manage promotional activities, record samples, and so forth. The bassist uses hers to e-mail her mom once a week, and otherwise it ends up collecting dust. See how one makes sense as a business deduction and the other doesn't? Or one actor is cast as a boxer and asked to "bulk up" by the director because he will be shirtless on stage and needs to look the part. His gym membership may be deductible (as a necessary expense to make the money he made on that gig) whereas another gym membership for an actor who is just working out "to stay fit" may not be.

- **Incorporating or Not:** This is a very complicated decision that, like making estimated payments, is a factor of many personal circumstances. The fact that one editor on a film has incorporated herself does not mean that it makes sense for every editor on the project. Keep focused on the important considerations discussed earlier in this book, and you will know you are in the right form of business for you. And if someone asks you why you are not set up as an LLC, you can simply respond, "I reviewed all the possibilities, and I'm set up in the way that works best for me."

WHAT TO DO IF YOU HAVE QUESTIONS

Everything clear? Crystal clear? Good.

But odds are good that even if you understand what you're reading, even if you keep up with the key points, and even if you can answer the study questions correctly, issues *still* might come up in the future that will leave you stumped. How do I apply this to my particular situation? What if what made sense for me in year one doesn't make any sense anymore now that I'm in year five? How do you address these questions?

Here are a few good strategies for getting help on the business end of your artistic career. I've tried to list them in the order I would approach them, but feel free to rearrange as suits your needs:

1. **Reach out to your team.** That's what they're there for: to help you take the rules and apply them to your situation. I don't know a whole lot about golf, but from what I can gather, even though it's the player who has to go through the work of swinging the club—and who gets the glory or suffers the humiliation of making or botching the shot—he or she still consults a caddy along the way to provide insights about the specifics of the course. That's like your team. Count on them to support you along the way.

2. **Contact industry or trade groups.** Some of these groups are most active online. Others are unions with physical offices and staff you can call. Even if they don't have the answer for you directly, they can often point you in the direction of the answer. Why? Because the issue you're facing was likely faced at least once before by someone else who does exactly what you do. These trade groups are excellent sources for connecting those experiences so you all don't keep making the same mistakes and can learn from your collective consciousness.

3. **Ask the IRS for guidance.** Full disclosure. The IRS can be a bear sometimes. When you pick up the phone and call in, you are often at the mercy of the mood of the person on the other end of the line. Sometimes it can go very well and be very helpful. Other times you will find someone who can't get past the notion that your nonprofit film association is deducting bags of popcorn as an advertising expense. But it's worth trying sometimes, because if you talk to the right person, there's nothing

better than getting it from the source. One thing to keep in mind: they will comment on your question over the phone, but you won't end up with a response in writing. To get that, you will need to request something called a private letter ruling, which is the IRS answering *your specific question* by official means. This letter ruling is then made public (with your name hidden), so everyone can learn from it and the IRS can avoid answering the same question over and over. A good CPA can help you search the letter rulings before requesting your own, since that process has some fees associated with it.

4. **Ask your competition.** This seems contradictory, but in today's economy, many have realized that it's not about "win at all costs," and a lot can be gained through what's called "competitive collaboration." Besides, you're not asking for the secrets to their design process or who they know that booked them in that great venue. You're asking how they categorize this or that kind of spending. And there's nothing wrong with sharing that kind of information. Just be mindful of the warnings in the last section about the kinds of advice that *are* dangerous to take from your peers. For those things, you should turn to a professional.

Study Questions

1. Who are the key players on your team?
2. What's the best way to find a service provider?
3. What are the four ongoing responsibilities you have, regardless of business structure?

Answers

1. Your CPA, attorney, and banker.
2. Personal referrals are the best way to find service providers you can trust.
3. Tracking income from all sources, keeping up with your expenses and tagging them with a category, interacting with your team, and planning for your tax payments.

WRAPPING IT UP

Asking for help is not admitting defeat. It's how you tackle this messy and confusing world of the business of being an artist. And that's a necessary component to maintaining your career as an artist or creative professional. Hopefully the tools and guidance you received by reading this book will give you some courage to stand up for yourself and to avoid being the victim of your own financial future. The idea here was never to get you to the point where you are expert enough to be able to do everything by yourself. That would take the kind of education that comes through years and years of study; just think, there probably aren't a lot of accountants or lawyers qualified to do what you do either. But I want to help you understand the value in thinking about how you set yourself up and the habits you build along the way—and to get you comfortable in the conversations you will have with your team. Remember, they are there to support you. You don't need to do it alone—even if you're a business of one. All the best, and much success to you in your career.

Index